Planning Your Piano Success

A Blueprint for Aspiring Musicians

STEWART GORDON

OXFORD
UNIVERSITY PRESS

UNIVERSITY PRESS

Oxford University Press is a department of the University of Oxford.
It furthers the University's objective of excellence in research, scholarship,
and education by publishing worldwide.

Oxford   New York
Auckland   Cape Town   Dar es Salaam   Hong Kong   Karachi
Kuala Lumpur   Madrid   Melbourne   Mexico City   Nairobi
New Delhi   Shanghai   Taipei   Toronto

With offices in
Argentina   Austria   Brazil   Chile   Czech Republic   France   Greece
Guatemala   Hungary   Italy   Japan   Poland   Portugal   Singapore
South Korea   Switzerland   Thailand   Turkey   Ukraine   Vietnam

Oxford is a registered trade mark of Oxford University Press
in the UK and certain other countries.

Published in the United States of America by
Oxford University Press
198 Madison Avenue, New York, NY 10016

Library of Congress Cataloging-in-Publication Data
Gordon, Stewart, 1930–
  Planning your piano success : a blueprint for aspiring musicians / Stewart Gordon.
    p.   cm.
Includes bibliographical references and index.
  ISBN 978-0-19-994244-2 (pbk. : alk. paper) — ISBN 978-0-19-994242-8 (hardcover : alk. paper)
  1. Pianists—Vocational guidance. 2. Pianists—Vocational guidance—Juvenile literature. I. Title.
  ML3795.G755 2014
  786.2023—dc23

                          2013022337

9780199942428
9780199942442 (pbk.)

9   8   7   6   5   4   3   2   1

Printed in the United States of America on acid-free paper

CONTENTS

Preface vii

1. The Bug Bites 1

2. Bringing Your Family On Board 9

3. Shopping for the Right Teacher 15

4. Balancing Everything 25

5. Building Technique 31

6. Exploring Skills 43

7. Developing Performance Chops 57

8. Using Your Mind 67

9. Creating Fantasy 81

10. Securing Memorization 91

11. Handling Rejection . . . and Success 101

12. Choosing Your College 111

13. Finding Your Way During the College Years 123

14. Planning Repertoire 131

15. Selecting Repertoire 137

16. Broadening Horizons 151

17. The Road Ahead 161

Annotated Selected Bibliography 165
Index 173

Over the years young pianists who want to become professional musicians and their parents have sought my counsel when they must make decisions or plan for the future. They seek advice for realizing short-term goals, such as finding a new music teacher or applying for college, as well as long-term assessments, such as degree of talent and probability for success in a competitive and often financially uncertain profession. In counseling the aspiring and their families, one is placed in the position of wanting to be both encouraging and realistic, to assist in taking the next steps, but also to sharpen perceptions as to the glories and challenges of their chosen career.

This book is an attempt to address in writing concerns that have surfaced often and to offer advice for building a career as a pianist and dealing with its challenges. In writing this book, I have tried to emphasize the excitement, nourishment, and inspiration musicians draw from their art, but also point to the difficulties and uncertainties that attend achievement and success. Hopefully, the former will outweigh the latter through these pages, so that those who read it will find inspiration, determination, and joy in pursuing their musical goals.

I wish to express appreciation to the host of wonderful young musicians whom I have counseled and taught through many decades. I attempt to advise and inspire them, but certainly they sustain and inspire me. I want to thank Todd Waldman and Lisbeth Redfield, my editors at Oxford University Press, who were patient and encouraging while this book grew from a short sketch to its present form. Finally, I want to thank my partner, Jonathan Christopher Reynolds, who is always patient with the professor when he sequesters himself to write yet another book.

Stewart Gordon
Claremont, California
August 2012

Planning Your Piano Success

The Bug Bites

You probably won't see a blinding flash of light or hear a clap of thunder. You may not even sense a realization that you can pinpoint in time. Indeed, its onset may be gradual. But at some point, you know that music is the center of your life, the one thing that brings you infinite inner joy and satisfaction. It is why you were born and what you want to do for the rest of your life.

Many other questions may surface at the same time. Do I have enough talent? Can I become good enough? Will I be able to support myself with what I want to do? These questions bother you, but they do not overwhelm you. You brush them aside, thinking you will deal with them later, or maybe you'll get lucky, or, more philosophically, if this is what you were meant to do, the rest will take care of itself.

You are not alone. Every generation has seen those for whom music is the reason for living. Every generation has had to face the same challenges, doubts, and insecurities. When you study the lives of great musicians of the past, you find that they too faced the questions you now face.

How did they do financially? A few were able to rise to the top of the financial ladder, to be regarded as rich. Most of them managed, often as well as most of the general population of their time. Even so, earning a living in the arts, whether it be in music or another artistic field, may mean that times of having plenty of money will be offset with periods of financial insecurity.

An example is Mozart. He remains one of the greatest geniuses in Western music. Indeed, he was admired and given lavish gifts as a child prodigy. As an adult he chose not to tie himself to the security of being in the service of a noble family, a source of income Haydn embraced. Thus Mozart was what we would call today a "freelance" musician for the most part. He had to piece together an income from performing, teaching, commissions for compositions, and grants. After he married and took on family responsibilities, he often had to worry over finances, and some of his letters contained requests to borrow money. Still, his family was provided for amply, and they moved in a society that was affluent and expensive. At the time of his death he had very few debts. It is well known that he was buried in a common grave, but such was a reflection of the custom of the time, not an indication that he was a pauper. The perception that he was poverty-stricken most of his life is an exaggeration some nineteenth-century historians put forward, possibly because the image of a starving genius seemed more "romantic" to them.

Some famous musicians started out well, but political changes threw their lives into upheaval, and they had to fight to exist. Beethoven enjoyed support from noble, rich families early in his career, but as Napoleon Bonaparte conquered Europe, many of those who helped Beethoven lost their fortunes.

Moreover, currency was devalued, so Beethoven's yearly grants were not worth as much, and he had to pinch pennies late in his career. Rachmaninoff had to start over in a new country with his family, all their possessions in suitcases, for he lost his home and his job as a result of Russia's Bolshevik revolution. Similarly, Bartók was out of favor with the Nazi regime that took over in his native Hungary, so he had to leave an area where his reputation was prestigious and start over in the United States, where he was relatively unknown.

Moreover, earning a livelihood as a musician may mean doing tasks that don't represent artistic expression. Bach had to meet job deadlines everywhere he worked, so he was not able to wait for "good" composing moods. Chopin taught Parisian socialites, some of whom were untalented. At one point Bartók—yes, him again—had to earn money by cataloging folk songs for a university library, a task that, although interesting to him, led to a period in which he composed but little. Although Schubert was trained to teach school, he was not good at it because he hated it, and he struggled with finances all of his short life.

One could cite many examples of great musicians who had to face difficult circumstances. But they were human beings, and life can be tough; it's not necessarily either easy or fair. But thankfully they stuck it out and continued to create, because the music they left behind enriches the world every day!

Consider the following story. A young musician traveled to an important cultural center. While he was there, friends and admirers persuaded him to make his debut. The event was announced in the local media, and he was heralded as a rising young pianist from a foreign country. He was very nervous about how he would be received, for he knew important people had been invited to the concert, people who could advance his career if they were impressed.

Here is a portion of the account he wrote home to his family:

The journalists have taken note of me; perhaps they'll trash me, but that's necessary to underline the praise. The stage manager of the theater, Demar, is very kind and amiable to me. He was so encouraging with his assurances before I went on to the stage, and kept my thoughts off of it so well that I was not very nervous, especially as the hall was not full. My friends and colleagues spread themselves over the hall to listen for opinions and criticisms. . . . Some lady said "A pity the boy has so little style." If that is all the fault anybody found—and otherwise they assure me that they heard only praises, and that they never started the bravos themselves—then I don't need to worry. . . . All the same it is being said everywhere that I play too softly, or rather, too delicately for people used to the piano-pounding of the artists here. I expect to find this reproach in the paper, especially as the editor's daughter thumps frightfully. It doesn't matter, there has always got to be a *but* somewhere, and I would rather it were that one than have people say I played too loud . . . I decided that if the papers so smash me that I could not again appear before the world, I would take to interior house painting[1]. . . .

Note the insecurity and worry in the letter, despite the fact that friends offered assurances of success. The point to be taken is that demons of doubt trouble virtually every musician. When you must deal with them, know that you are not alone and that having to face them does not indicate any lack of talent. Incidentally, the date of that letter was August 12, 1829, and the young man who wrote it was Frederic Chopin.

There are also all the ones we don't know about, because they didn't go down in the annals of music history. These people could form an army. They had varying levels of talent, but they were individuals who loved music and dedicated their lives to it. Although they are no longer remembered, they were once part of an important body that made up the musical culture of their day. Each in his or her own way contributed to the vitality and continuity of the art, and without them the art would have been undernourished and might have died.

Such observations bring us to the big uncertainty every aspiring musician has to face. Different people may frame it in different words, but it is always there. Do I have enough talent? Am I good enough? Will I measure up to the best around me? Will I make it? Am I starting too late? Finding assurance that you can become one of the best is a quest that gnaws at everyone. Sometimes its intensity may be as potent as the love for music itself.

---

1. Adapted from The Letters of Chopin, collected by Henryk Opienski, translated by E. L. Voynich, Dover, New York, 1988, pp. 53–5.

Well, you know what? It's an issue you will have to deal with but won't ever be able to resolve fully. It's part of the gig. It's like answering "Am I pretty enough to be a beauty queen?," "Am I strong enough to make it to the Olympics?," "Will I meet the right person, fall in love and get married and live happily ever after?," "Will I live a good enough life to get into heaven?"

You're talented. Surely people have told you that just as, in the examples, folks comment on how pretty someone is, or insist you'll meet your soul mate someday, or talk about a relative being in heaven when everyone knows that person had both good and bad qualities. Such examples are all around us and reflect that no one can be certain about his or her destiny. And such realization helps mitigate insecurity. Even so, these thoughts may not be enough to satisfy you.

Just face it. Your question is impossible to answer because no one can predict your future with certainty, not you or anyone else. If you are passionate about music and becoming a musician, you must wade in, do your best, and have faith that good things will follow. Also remember that many seers believe positive attitudes go a long way toward producing positive circumstances. Indeed, subscribing to that philosophy, setting your goals, and achieving your best is about all you or anyone else can do. But such an attitude needn't unnerve you, for, as the next chapter will point out, risk attends many professions, not just music.

Up to now, we've considered only the scary part, which is indeed the order in which we humans often think. But there's the good stuff too. There's the fact that you will fill your life with something that excites you. You will bask in vitality generated by your creativity, an energy that will sustain you through the years ahead and make you feel that every day is worth living. You will bask in a world of color, imagination, and magic, one that is intellectually satisfying, emotionally fulfilling, and spiritually sensitive.

Regard yourself as lucky. You need only look around to see a host of people who spend their lives doing something they are never passionate about. They endure the work they do, count the hours and days before every vacation, and long for retirement. Because you are a musician, you are not among them. Be grateful.

Most musicians live, eat, and breathe music. They anticipate the next project, perfect the next performance, engage the next audience, and strive to grow musically every day. At the end of their life span, they typically wish for more years in which to continue their romance with the muse. The excitement never wanes. The thrill never ends. The love deepens. The satisfaction is unmatched and infinite. If such sentiments seem high-flown, read the comments of a few famous musicians about their art:

- The aim and final end of all music should be none other than the glory of God and the refreshment of the soul. Johann Sebastian Bach (1685–1750)
- I despise a world which does not feel that music is a higher revelation than all wisdom and philosophy. Ludwig van Beethoven (1770–1827)
- Love cannot express the idea of music, while music may give an idea of love. Hector Berlioz (1803–1869)
- Music is an outburst of the soul. Frederick Delius (1862–1934)
- Music is enough for a lifetime, but a lifetime is not enough for music. Sergei Rachmaninoff (1873–1943)
- I've never known a musician who regretted being one. Whatever deceptions life may have in store for you, music itself is not going to let you down. Virgil Thomson (1896–1989)
- To stop the flow of music would be like the stopping of time itself, incredible and inconceivable. Aaron Copland (1900–1990)
- Music creates order out of chaos: for rhythm imposes unanimity upon the divergent, melody imposes continuity upon the disjointed, and harmony imposes compatibility upon the incongruous. Yehudi Menuhin (1916–1999)

Philosophers and thinkers have also pondered the wonder of music and its effects for centuries:

- Music in the soul can be heard by the universe. Lao Tzu (b. 6th century B.C.)

- Music produces a kind of pleasure which human nature cannot do without. Confucius (551–479 B.C.)
- Music is a moral law. It gives soul to the universe, wings to the mind, flight to the imagination, and charm and gaiety to life and to everything. Plato (428–348 B.C.)
- Music is God's gift to man, the only art of Heaven given to earth, the only art of earth we take to Heaven. Walter Savage Landor, English writer (1775–1864)
- Music expresses that which cannot be said and on which it is impossible to remain silent. Victor Hugo (1802–1885)
- Music takes us out of the actual and whispers to us dim secrets that startle our wonder as to who we are, and for what, whence, and whereto. Ralph Waldo Emerson (1803–1882)
- Where words fail, music speaks. Hans Christian Andersen (1805–1875)
- Music is the universal language of mankind. Henry Wadsworth Longfellow (1807–1882)
- When I hear music, I fear no danger, I am invulnerable. I see no foe. I am related to the earliest of times, and to the latest. Henry David Thoreau (1817–1862)
- Without music, life would be an error. Friedrich Nietzsche (1844–1900)
- Music is the language of the spirit. It opens the secret of life bringing peace, abolishing strife. Kahlil Gibran Lebanese-born American philosophical essayist and poet (1883–1931)

Notice that when you think in these terms, answers to questions about the strength of your talent or the extent of your success become relatively unimportant. What's important is that you are among the most favored of human beings, for you have been bitten by the bug. Your life will never be the same again. Be grateful and rejoice. Then dig in and work. And trust your deepest inner convictions. Always trust.

2

Bringing Your Family On Board

Parents almost always want the best for their children. They stand by to counsel offspring, gently nudging toward wise decisions or forcibly imposing directions believed to reap long-term benefits. Moreover, they sometimes regard the dreams of their children as passing fancies, and, indeed, not without reason. Children may dream of becoming figures in their fantasy world: princes, princesses, superheroes, or space travelers. These goals often change with maturity.

When you share your dream of becoming a musician with your parents, you may encounter any number of reactions. These stem from their concern for your well-being, how much they share your enthusiasm for music, and their experience with the profession. Had you been Johann Sebastian Bach, Mozart, Czerny, Liszt, or Brahms, this part would have been easy, for being a musician was a family tradition. No need to explain anything. If you are lucky enough to have a family of some affluence, such as Mendelssohn or Poulenc, you may find less parental concern about

possible remuneration from a career in music. Parents who value intellectual or artistic endeavors, such as those of Schubert and Clementi, often
value their child's talent and arrange support for its development. Still
other parents resisted. The fathers of Robert Schumann and Igor Stravinsky insisted their sons go to law school. Alexander Gretchaninov had to
enter the Moscow conservatory secretly, for his father expected his son to
take over the family business.

If you have to defend choosing music as your profession because of
uncertain financial returns, you can argue that in today's rapidly changing
times, almost no profession is immune from ups and downs. In the 1990s
the dot-com world was considered recession proof. In 2000 it collapsed as
the early thirst for computer technology was quenched and a more normal
rate of assimilation took over. Indeed, professions based on technology
seem sure-fire at first glance, but change is so rapid that keeping up demands that those in technology fields enlist as much creativity and agility as anyone in the arts. Moreover, the recession of the early twenty-first
century has subjected many "solid" professions to hard times: real estate,
investment brokers, small business entrepreneurs, restaurants, hospitality
and travel enterprises, to mention only a few. Bad weather can ruin farm
crops. Oil spills set back entire industries.

Have musicians fared less well in a depressed economy? Perhaps, but
consider the amount of music that is consumed in our society. Music surrounds us. It is an integral part of most of our entertainment: concert presentations, of course, but also movies, television, computer games. Music
is an important part of most religious services. Almost every individual
has a personal list of musical favorites, and listening to these for pleasure
goes on constantly. Think how many musical downloads take place every
hour!

Moreover, participating in musical activities is a satisfying form of
emotional release. Thus, playing or creating music becomes an avenue of
personal expression. As a result, students still study piano. Parents still
pay for piano lessons. Music competitions and festivals at all levels continue to flourish. Schools continue to teach music classes and offer music
curricula.

It is logical to assume that inasmuch as music is ubiquitous in our society, you ought to be able to find a way to earn your livelihood from it. This is, indeed, true! Still, there are several keys to being able to tap into this richness. First, you need to envision yourself as a complete musician, not merely a pianist who plays classical music. This translates into developing a complete set of skills during the time you get your musical education. Second, it means using your imagination to relate what you do to the culture you live in. Creative ideas in this area may not come easily or rapidly, but if you persist, breakthroughs will certainly take place. Finally, it means learning how to market yourself and casting aside the natural hesitation you may feel for selling yourself as a musician to a broad segment of the population. All of these keys are discussed in detail in later chapters in this book.

The argument is often heard that more money can be made in other professions, perhaps in the legal, medical, or business worlds. On the superstar level, hardly, for musical superstars are often popular icons whose earnings are in the same league with those of the most famous athletes and actors. Still, one must grant that the rank and file of some other professions often earn more dollars for their time than do musicians. We expect to pay more for medical and legal counsel than we do for piano lessons. But musicians are in good company, for we also do not pay our ministers or teachers as well as our lawyers or doctors.

Indeed, some musicians have eschewed relying on musical activities as a primary means of support. Often their reasoning is that by providing for themselves and their families by doing something else, they can keep their musical activities free from practical considerations and possibly commercial influences. They exchange the time robbed from musical activities to earn a living for purity and independence. One of the best-known examples of this philosophy is the career of the American composer, Charles Ives (1874–1954). He knew he wanted to write music that was experimental, ahead of its time, and not within the scope of current popular taste. He sold insurance for a living and created the music he wanted to create. In his case, the arrangement worked well, for he is considered one of the great pioneers of the early twentieth century, and many of his compositions not only are important historically but also are part of the ongoing classical repertoire.

For many musicians, pursuing another profession or being a musician was not an either/or choice. Rather, they had periods of doing both. Russian composer Nicolai Rimsky-Korsakov (1844–1908) and French composer Albert Roussel (1864–1937) were both naval officers for a period of time. Many famous contemporary musicians earned degrees or worked in other fields that they felt contributed to the creativity of their musical endeavors. Karlheinz Stockhausen (1938–2007) was as interested in philosophy, aesthetics, and linguistics as in composing in the years of his education. Iannis Xenakis (1922–2001) got a degree in civil engineering and worked in an architectural firm in Paris while pursuing his career as a composer.

In talking with your parents you may want to use the "money isn't everything" argument. Surely one wants to earn enough to live comfortably, but loving your work counts for something. In fact, musicians typically love their work so much that they eschew retirement, often continuing to earn an income as long as they are able to sustain professional activity. Such dedication to one's work is acknowledged even by those who do not understand the degree of passion musicians have for their profession. Moreover, parents usually want their children to be happy above all, so making such a point may, indeed, sway them, provided, of course, they believe you are in for the long haul.

Once you bring your parents around to the point of embracing, perhaps cautiously, your wish to become a professional musician, begin to strengthen their support by drawing them into your world. First and foremost, be prepared to perform for them, family members, and friends at all times. Have something ready to go. Do not stand behind such excuses as "I haven't practiced today" or "Everything is too new." Family and friends do not understand these excuses, just as they do not understand the challenge each performance may pose for you as a developing musician. Your refusal to play is apt to be interpreted at best as never being ready and at worst as temperament. It is up to you to anticipate occasions on which you may be asked to play and be ready for them.

Seek opportunities to show what you can do in areas that are important to your parents. Perhaps you can volunteer a performance for a special church service or to raise funds for a service organization your parents support. Urge your parents to attend your teacher's studio recitals in which you are playing. If this event is presented on a professional level, your parents should be both proud and impressed. (See the next chapter on teacher shopping.) They will become acclimated to the profession you want to pursue and be drawn into it. Similarly, plan to involve them in music festivals, master classes, or adjudicated events at which you play. Most music teachers belong to professional organizations that stage these events regularly throughout the year. Written comments from guest evaluators at these events are usually positive and encouraging, and these will strengthen your image as a young musician in your parents' thinking.

Finding time for such activities may, indeed, take time away from practicing that special piece you want to learn, or working on your technique. Realize that you cannot forgo these ancillary demands. Being a complete musician . . . a community musician . . . an active musician should always play a role in your musical career, and it is often challenging to balance your personal musical goals with your broader musical commitments. Indeed, you may find yourself working overtime to squeeze everything in, but such intense activity is a hallmark of the professional musician's life, and you can find satisfaction in the pleasure your music gives to those around you.

Once your parents and family members understand the culture that surrounds your development as a professional musician, chances are they will support it with pride and enthusiasm. To be sure, they may harbor fear that the road ahead will be bumpy, the competition fierce, and financial returns not as forthcoming as they might hope. But they will know that you are doing what you want to do with your life. Added to that knowledge will be the satisfaction that comes from learning to understand and appreciate your world. Indeed, they will probably end up being the most ardent supporters of your endeavors and bask in the glow of each of your successes.

3

Shopping for the Right Teacher

This discussion may impress you as being heartless. If you are like most students who enjoy studying and playing the piano, you love and trust your piano teacher. You would never entertain the idea that your piano teacher wasn't the best choice for you, and you would feel that you are betraying a loved one by shopping for someone else. These sentiments are understandable and laudable. But consider the following.

If you suspected you were gifted enough in a sport to aspire to the professional level, when would you start training for that reach? When would you seek evaluation and guidance from someone who had knowledge of the big-time leagues? You suspect that if you waited until you were out of high school, it would probably be too late. Or if not too late, late enough to make achieving your goal a lot harder.

Now you may be lucky enough to be with a big-league trainer already. So if your piano teacher measures up, then stay where you are. Even so, if your goal is to become a professional musician, you need to apply some tests to your teacher to determine if you are getting the training you need. This is not betrayal, just intelligent, long-range career planning.

Start by evaluating the caliber of students who are studying with your teacher. You should be able to identify at least two or three who already play like you want to play, who win awards in local competitions, and who garner praise from all sides. These are signs that your talented peers have had faith in your teacher and that their work together is producing results. If their playing provides examples you can look up to, generates occasional twinges of envy, or makes you sweat to hold your own in the studio environment, fine. You are with a teacher who attracts and trains the best, and that is where you should be.

Most teachers are active in professional organizations and have students playing in festivals and competitions on a regular basis. Not every entrant can be a winner or place highly every time, but assuming your teacher has students competing regularly, recognition should be forthcoming from time to time. How do you know who else studies with your teacher or how their performances fare? You should make it your business to cultivate a social interface with others who study with your teacher at student recitals, theory classes, competitions, or festivals. Being friendly and garnering knowledge of your professional environment is a good habit to form. It leads to awareness and respect for both your work and that of others.

Some teachers may not place a high value on competitions. If you find this to be the case with your teacher, there should still be opportunities to perform and to hear others perform regularly. Thus your teacher should present student recitals every few months at which parents and friends can come to hear you and others. These events should be well organized, and the performances presented should be secure and musically enjoyable. Memory slips and technical breakdowns can happen to anyone, but if your teacher is effective, the recital should not be rife with problematic performances. There should be regular performing opportunities within your teacher's studio, get-togethers where students play for one another. These may offer opportunities to test performance of works that are still in progress. If that is the case, performances may not always be as polished, but as you attend these sessions, you should be able to note progress and improvement in everyone.

These are some of the outward signs of your teacher's professionalism. You also need to think about how your teacher is handling your personal growth, checking to see if you are getting what you need from your teacher. To do this, ask yourself the following questions. Be honest in your answers, but also be careful when you answer not to attribute your own deficiencies to your teacher. Even the best teacher can only lead, prescribe, and inspire. You are still responsible for following through and getting the work done. Now here are areas to consider and some questions to answer.

Technique: Has your teacher laid out a technical regimen for you, and is it working? A satisfactory answer to this question consists of more than assigning technical studies such as those of Czerny or exercises such as ones by Hanon or Dohnányi. If such material is used, does your teacher both hear it and suggest ways it can be used to develop your technique? Does your teacher talk about the use of the fingers, hands, wrists, arms, and torso and its effect on musical results? Does your teacher help you solve technique problems in repertoire by offering explicit practice instructions? Does your teacher guide you through these instructions at your lessons? Does your teacher make suggestions for maintaining a healthy physical approach to the keyboard? Has your teacher been successful in helping you alleviate tension problems you might encounter?

Touch and Tone: Almost a century ago, a controversy raged as to whether or not the piano was capable of a *qualitative* variety of tone. Physicists went to great lengths to prove that it was not, and pianists everywhere took issue because these findings seemed to contradict what their ears told them: that different tone "qualities" were discernible and pianists had individual "sounds," just as singers have discernible differences in voices. The answer to this apparent contradiction was simply that what pianists perceive as "quality" is a combination of many other factors: degrees of noise and percussion in producing the tone (surface and key bed noises); the type of impact generated when the hammer strikes the string, the speed with which the hammer falls away from the string as well as the distance it falls before it comes to rest; dynamic relationships between tones, both vertically (in chords) and horizontally (in lines); degrees of connection between tones (legato, portato, staccato, etc.); and use of the piano's pedals. So in this context, you should ask yourself these questions. Does your teacher talk about tone production and various touches used in different musical contexts? Have you ever been given exercises to develop your tone? Does your teacher show you several ways in which you can produce tone in any given context?

Practice Habits. Has your teacher outlined practice procedures for you, as well as offered suggestions for practicing in specific styles and pieces? Has your teacher discussed how to use your practice time wisely, how to pace yourself, how to focus, and how to generate creativity? Does your teacher ask questions at your lessons to check your practice routines, procedures, and effectiveness?

Repertoire: Do you believe that your teacher has an extensive knowledge of repertoire and styles? Are you hearing a lot of different repertoire as your encounter performances by others in your teacher's studio? Does your teacher assign you a wide variety of repertoire and styles? Is some of the repertoire challenging without being out of reach? Are you encouraged to explore new repertoire on your own? Is there any repertoire you feel your teacher is not comfortable teaching?

Performance: Does your teacher encourage you to perform? Does your teacher offer specific advice to help deal with the stress leading up to performance? If your performance is memorized, has your teacher showed you how to memorize securely, helped you set up a memorization schedule, and checked your memorization effectiveness? Are your performances successful? When they fall short (as they do with everyone from time to time), does your teacher help you evaluate and give you specific ways to overcome the shortcomings?

Collaboration: Does your teacher provide opportunities for you to collaborate with other musicians? Does your teacher coach such collaboration? Is such collaboration part of recital presentations or other performance activities?

Theoretical Studies: Does your teacher provide theory, ear training, and analysis classes? If not (many teachers do not have time to schedule them), does your teacher encourage such training as part of your musical development and suggest where you can get it?

Ancillary Skills: Has your teacher planned a sight-reading schedule with you? Does your teacher teach you how to improvise? Does your teacher check your progress in these skills at least periodically?

All those questions add up to a tall order. But you have a tall-order goal, so you need to ask them and think about why these aspects of your training are important. Remember your teacher doesn't have to score perfectly to be the right teacher for you at this stage of your development. You may, in fact, decide that you have no time for theory classes at this point in your life, or that collaboration can happen only occasionally, perhaps due to practical considerations like difficulties in scheduling or arranging transportation. Whatever is missing now will have to be addressed at some point. Still, limitations may exist. So in asking these questions about your teacher, use reason.

On the other hand, if this examination brings you to the realization that you are not getting the kind of detailed guidance you need, week in and week out, then you should consider moving to a teacher who can provide it. This change need not be effected abruptly or without consideration of the good work your present teacher has done. Still, you should begin to research other teachers, planning the change well in advance and hopefully at a natural time break, such as during a summer hiatus. Such a plan includes taking steps to see if the teacher you target will accept you at an appropriate time.

So how do you know whom to approach? Do your research. Attend recitals of competition winners and learn who is teaching the outstanding pianists who impress you. Pull up the websites of music teacher organizations to find the names of peers who are honored at various events. Their teachers are usually noted. Make a list of the teachers whose students are honored often. Ask other pianists you admire about their teachers, gathering information as to teaching content and style. Be sure to ask about regular availability, because some well-known teachers are too busy to see students regularly, and you may be at a point where you need carefully scheduled guidance.

When you make an appointment with a prospective new teacher, be prepared to play at a level that represents your best work. When your prospective teacher asks about your present situation, be honest in describing your current or previous teacher, what your goals are, and what you seek at this stage of your development. You are smart enough to be both honest and tactful. Above all, do not let the anticipation of starting with a new teacher tempt you to bad-mouth your old teacher.

Changing teachers is a sensitive issue for both your old and new teachers. The teacher you leave may be hurt when told that you are moving on. The teacher you approach may feel an ethical issue is at stake, perhaps not accepting you until you break with your former teacher. Your prospective teacher may advise you to wait, moving at the right time in the right way. The change may not take place until a normal break in studying, such as at the end of the school year or after a performance that represents a culmination of your work with your present teacher. Despite this sensitivity, changes take place frequently. Old teachers recover and new teachers eventually feel you are "free" enough to become one of their students.

You may have to face being turned down by the teacher of your choice. Good teachers are in great demand, so they have the option of accepting only those students who interest them. Some teachers accept only students they perceive as being at a certain level of achievement, and the teacher you audition for may feel you aren't there yet. Some teachers try to assess the musical instincts of prospective students and accept only those they deem "talented." Such assessments are subjective, and they should be taken for exactly what they are: quickly formed personal opinions. Mistakes are often made, and opinions among professionals vary widely. Finally, codes of ethics sometimes result in complex relationships between professionals, so your targeted teacher may feel uncomfortable about accepting anyone who studies with your present teacher.

Being turned down by a teacher does not alter the evaluation of your present teacher or your decision to move on. Simply go back to the drawing board and target another teacher who meets the criteria you have set up. Once you are accepted by a new teacher, be prepared to forgo entering competitive events for a period of time. Many organizations require study with a teacher for several months before allowing participation in such events. If you encounter such restrictions, be patient and use the time to become accustomed to your new teacher and master newly assigned repertoire.

William Kapell (1922–1953) was one of the most celebrated pianists of the mid-twentieth century. His brilliant career was cut short when he was killed in the crash of a commercial airline. His teacher, Olga Samaroff was one of the most powerful teachers at the Juilliard School of Music in New York City. She was known to her students affectionately as "madam." She was responsible for taking Kapell from a talented boy to a mature artist. As he was embarking on his meteoric rise, she wrote to him about her musical and teaching ideals in a letter that is both touching and revealing:

March 28, 1947

Dear Willy:

It was truly a wonderful experience last night to hear your records and to realize the big step forward you have taken in the direction you most needed progress, namely, tone. Never lose that beautiful voice again.

If you listen every minute and ask it of yourself and *realize that you know how* your playing will always have this quality which is so rare and so necessary to great music.

I want to wind up our various discussions during the past ten days with the following thoughts: You spoke last night, and believe me I appreciated it deeply, of the "concept" I had given you of the Chopin sonata and other works. I am happy you feel that way, and yet as a teacher with long experience and a certain intuitive insight which I believe has enabled me to get the results I have gotten with talents of such different types, I want to point out to you that these concepts of single compositions are far the *least* I have given you.

Without your being fully aware of it throughout the years you have absorbed the things that every interpreter needs and that make a pianist an artist.

1. The capacity to recognize in a score the essence of the music.

2. A sense of form, including harmonic structure plus feeling.

3. A sense of phrasing, including different levels.

4. A clarified concept of different types of touch, i.e., legato, staccato, portamento, and non-legato, especially the rightly fingered *true* legato line.

5. The reality of a dynamic scheme ranging from a triple pianissimo to a triple fortissimo, and the pedaling that is so all-important to sound.

6. The various degrees of accents ranging from the strong beat of the bar to a double sforzando.

7. How to find tempo through the application of whatever indication the composer gives to the pulse unit in the bar.

8. The capacity to recognize the *significance* of all these printed things which so many people either ignore or take for granted.

9. The realization that every artist must be able to go beyond the printed page through imagination, instinct, and capacity for emotion.

10. A method of work that insures memory and mastery. The kind of work that achieves not just notes but the way the notes should be played so that the player is not wasting a major part of his life establishing the habit of playing music the way he does not intend to perform it.

11. A sense of ensemble which was developed in you primarily through your second piano playing of concertos and which has made you an outstanding ensemble soloist with orchestras.

12. The road to enrichment of the mind through reading and outside experiences which are absolutely necessary if an artist is not to be egocentric, ingrowing, and limited as a human being.

Believe me, Willy dear, *these* things are infinitely more important than any concept of any single piece. Probably any teacher would claim the teaching of these big basic things in music but the ability to make them significant to the student is apparently rare because hardly any student comes to me with such concepts in any clarified form.

It is only through a constant insistence on the part of the teacher for *independent work* that finally develops in the student the capacity to handle these things himself. If there is any secret to my teaching I believe this is it.

The above mentioned things are those that will enable you to go forward independently all your life into the study of all kinds of music because, as I said to you last night, style really lies in the way the music is written and our *understanding* of all the elements that go to make it up is the thing that will enable us to approach *any* style with sureness.

It is valuable to know traditions and God knows we have enough opportunity to do that through reading, listening to records, and performances at concerts, but the only traditions that have real value are those that make the music live as the composer intended it should be.

The fact that my big pupils, by that I mean pupils of big talent, are able to go on growing after they leave me as Tureck [Rosalyn Tureck 1914–2003] has, as Battista (Joseph Battista 1918–1968) is doing, as you are doing, proves that this way of teaching plants the seeds for a whole artistic future.

A teacher who only provides a limited repertory of coached or imitative interpretations gives the student the easiest way to an immediate result but limits him terribly in his independent approach to a wide field.

With regard to your program for next year, I would hate to see you play the Bach-Liszt Fantasy and Fugue. These noisy transcriptions of Bach organ music are terribly dated and will re-stamp you, if one can use such a word, in the type-cast direction many people are inclined to attribute to your work.

Also, as I said last night, I truly believe that the new music you take up at this point beginning work on it at a much higher level than you had before will produce wonderful results. It will mean hard work but as you seem fit it seems to me this is the right time to undertake a flight into the unknown and see what you can do with things that are in no way influenced by the various phases you have gone through during the past six years.

Good luck to you and "knock them cold" in Chicago.

Yours devotedly,

"Madam"

P.S. It is the knowledge of what you possess *basically* that gives me such confidence in your ever-growing capacities as an artist. Never forget or neglect any of them. They form the musical treasures you and I piled up together.

—Permission to reprint Olga Samaroff's letter to William Kapell
was kindly given by the Piano Archives of the University of Maryland,
College Park, the home of the Kapell papers.

4

Balancing Everything

The adventure of becoming a professional musician is infinitely rewarding. You are blessed with passion. You get to do what you want to do in life. Even so, the muse makes severe demands on those who want to serve her. Since you love music, her demands do not seem outrageous, but they are, nonetheless, all-consuming.

Your entire life must be built around being the best musician you can be. Of course, there will be nonmusical events in your life that are significant. Even so, everything you do or experience will be in the context of your musical persona. This fact is at once exhilarating and frustrating. You will have to set your priorities, ration your time, and make continuing adjustments to balance normal living with a passion that constantly demands more attention and is never totally satisfied.

Since this is the case, you must teach yourself to enjoy this balancing act. On one side of the equation there is music, practicing, performing, and creating. On the other side is everything else. If preserving this balance is to work efficiently, you need to form the habit of thinking about it positively and applying a few simple principles.

First, build a schedule that includes everything you need to get done, with practicing at its center. It is important to identify when and where you will work each week. Once you have set up the times and places, regard these as important events, like appointments that must be met faithfully, not to be broken under normal circumstances. As you set up this schedule, leave yourself some wiggle room, for delays will undoubtedly occur and adjustments will have to be made.

Why the wiggle room? Well, we live in a world where things often go awry. When they do, extra time is needed to take care of the situation. You encounter unusually heavy traffic. You misplace your keys. You spill something. You have to deal with inclement weather. The wiggle room will help keep you from feeling like you are falling behind. If things go so smoothly that the wiggle room isn't really needed, then use it to do something pleasant, like taking a coffee or exercise break, not to add another ten minutes to your practice time.

If life gangs up on you and you do fall behind, be philosophical, staying as cool as possible. Remember that it was you who set up the schedule, so you are in command. It is easy to start regarding your schedule with a do-or-die attitude, one that leads to counterproductive frustration and tension. If you find that life's delays create a constant stream of frustrations, then it is quite possible you miscalculated and created a schedule that is too "tight." If you suspect this to be the case, take time to adjust your expectations.

The secret to handling a schedule effectively is to remain flexible enough to stay calm when upsets occur, but to pick up the schedule as soon as things settle down. Moreover, if you find you are running behind, resist the temptation to throw up your hands and forgo trying to pick up where you left off. Do not convince yourself that today's delays resulted in such a mess that you cannot make use of whatever time remains, or that you should wait until tomorrow to start over again. Indeed, tomorrow may present yet another set of frustrations, so it is best to do whatever you can with whatever time is left today.

Moreover, learning to use small segments of time to get something done is valuable for several reasons. First, these small windows of time add up, so that taken together they can be used to produce a significant amount of work. Second, you develop the mental agility to pick up where you left off easily and quickly. And finally, jumping into the middle of work sometimes generates a new perspective that offers useful insights.

When planning your schedule, be sure to reserve some time for yourself, for watching television, reading, surfing the net, playing with the dog, or whatever gives you pleasure. These periods will be limited, of course, because they are not the focal point of your life, but they are important for the longevity of your more serious goals. Without them you will go stale in the main arena, no matter how strongly you are motivated.

Above all, put into your schedule time for physical activity of some sort, be it exercising, walking, swimming, playing ball, or even practicing yoga. When you sit at the piano, you are making specific, complex demands on your body. You are striving to achieve goals that involve coordinating your sensory perceptions, complicated mental processes, neural signals, and muscular responses. The intensity of this process produces fatigue and tension.

Since this intense activity is focused mostly on the upper body, you are likely to feel fatigue or tension in your back, neck, arms, hands, or fingers. Some activity that provides exercise for the whole body offsets this focus and offers release for its tension. Thus whole-body exercise in some form should be a regular part of your lifestyle. Remember that the excellence of your performance as a musician is directly dependent on your physical well-being, so keeping yourself in shape is a must.

Now let's consider the practice time itself. You have set aside this block of time each day for your development as a musician, so you should think about how you are going to use it most effectively. Some just wade in each day without much preplanning. Others try to think about their practice time, but feel they don't know how to use it effectively.

Start your planning by considering how you will ration the time. If you practice warmup or technical exercises, know approximately how much time you plan to devote to this activity. If you have several repertoire items to cover, decide about how much time you will give to each. You needn't be rigid with these allotments at any point, but having guidelines will serve to address the material you need to cover. If you have a performance coming up, plan a time when you practice a nonstop rehearsal of the performance you will soon have to give.

Within each practice session, ask yourself what goals you would like to achieve in a given segment. This goal setting should remain flexible, because we don't always progress as fast as we would like. Conversely, sometimes goals fall into place more easily than we expect. Still, knowing what you want to get done is better than practicing without purpose. So whether it is drilling a hard technical spot, memorizing a section, or trying to pull a performance together conceptually, have something in mind as you begin to work.

Goal setting will often result in altering or ditching a habitual procedure because it has outlived its effectiveness. Be on the lookout for those points at which you need to change practice patterns. For example, when you first began learning a piece, you probably started at its beginning. Later you probably found that some parts need more work than others. Thus, you changed your focus and no longer always work from the beginning of the piece.

You may focus on improving one aspect of a work for a period of time, but stay sensitive to when your mind needs refreshing or other aspects of the music need attention. For example, you may have set up drills designed to address the technical challenges of a work. At some point your mind will tire of the repetitiveness of this activity. You may realize you are drilling mechanically, and technical improvement has all but stopped. At this point focus on some other aspect of the piece and come back to the technical challenge after a break. Turn to a detailed examination of musical challenges such as articulation, phrasing, structure, or dynamics. You may want to just sit and think about the piece, trying to pinpoint and internalize its emotional meaning.

Moreover, when you focus intensely on one aspect of a piece, be sure some other aspect is not being eroded in the process. For example, drilling technical passages slowly and deliberately may enhance security, but be watchful that the drill does not compromise such aspects as rhythmic precision, articulation, or dynamic nuance. Sometimes, one may forgo incorporating all musical demands of a passage in order to concentrate on one or another aspect of it. This setting aside the challenge of meeting all the demands of a passage should be limited to short periods of time, however, to avoid establishing a permanent warp in the complex relationship of its elements.

Your practice sessions may often consist of constantly adjusting and balancing. On one hand, you may need to concentrate on a goal until you sense measurable progress, but on the other, you may need switch to another goal if you sense you are in a rut. Happily, the work you do in a given area often germinates when you are focused on other things. Thus when you return to a given passage after a hiatus, you may be pleasantly surprised at how much it has improved.

Relegate some part of your brain to the job of being sure every minute you are practicing is productive. This vigilance is important, for it is easy to fall into time-consuming patterns that produce little result. Most pianists know these patterns well and try to avoid them: playing through a piece without much involvement, repetitious drilling without concentration, not stopping to correct details or address problems that appear, often with the thought you will attend to corrections later. Rather, try to imagine yourself as an orchestral conductor with limited time in which to rehearse. Every moment must count for something. Every repetition must leave an impression. Every concept must be crystallized.

And finally, with all of this going on in your head, you must remind yourself constantly that all your work has to add up to an artistic expression. Such would seem obvious, of course. But just as we must prompt ourselves to keep things in perspective when the highs and lows of life overtake us, we must also seek perspective with our musical work. Thus we should constantly impress on our consciousness that technique, drill, repetition, and all musical directions must coalesce with our own experience and emotional makeup to emerge as an expression of the beauty and wonder of the music itself.

5

Building Technique

Several important concepts attend developing the kind of technique you need to work successfully in the professional world. First, you have to relish the idea of developing super chops. Look around at other arenas of performance. If you go for the gold in any major sport, doing whatever it takes to get yourself prepared is taken for granted. If you want to change the world by discovering something in your lab, you expect to devote however many hours of work it takes to get your results. If you are determined to win your case in court, you don't count the cost in time and effort devoted to preparation. You just do it.

In short, there shouldn't be any question about working hard to develop your performance technique. Any attitude that even hints at doing just enough to get by will undermine achieving your best and attaining a level that ensures success. The question should not be whether or not to embark on a technical regime, but only which ones to adopt.

The technical programs you choose should address many different technical challenges, and you should move from any given one to the next in kaleidoscopic rotation. For example, if you ask, "Should I practice scales, arpeggios, and all that traditional stuff?," the answer is "Of course, but bring playing this material to a fluent level and move to something else." Playing this material is like mastering basic vocabulary when learning a language. You nail it down, start using it, and go on to something more complex.

Here is a list of this basic material:

- All major and minor scales (all forms) in two-, three-, and four-octave parallel segments, incorporating contrary motion as well
- All major and minor scales in thirds, sixths, and tenths (single notes in each hand)
- All major and minor arpeggios, all inversions, four octaves up and back
- Some routine built on arpeggios of various types of seventh chords: major/major, major/minor, minor/minor, half-diminished, diminished on all twelve pitches
- All major and minor scales in double notes: thirds, sixths, and octaves
- Chromatic scales parallel, contrary, and both minor and major double thirds, sixths, and octaves

Bring your imagination to bear when practicing material such as this. After the basic pattern becomes fluent, add dynamics, touch forms, right hand (R.H.) or left hand (L.H.) voicing. Cécile Genhart (1899–1983), a famous piano teacher of the Eastman School of Music for many years, challenged her students by asking for scales in polyrhythms: two in the L.H. against three in the R.H., then switch, as well as the more difficult three in the L.H.; and four in the R.H., and switch. She was also fond of what she lovingly called "Bartók scales," playing different scales in each hand simultaneously. Examples would be C major in the L.H. with E major in the R.H., or C minor in the L.H. with F-sharp major in the R.H. The list of similar possible combinations is extensive.

Practicing this material offers distinct benefits despite its reputation for being boring. You can focus on the physical process itself without having to incorporate many other elements that are inherent in playing compositions, but not necessary in this type of drill. Here you don't have to psych out composers' markings or expressive intentions. You can devote your entire concentration to fingering, coordination, touch, and tone. Once you get patterns going, you can add your own musical challenges.

A corollary of this narrowness is that you can watch and sense what you are doing physically, focus that is particularly helpful if you are trying to alter or expand your relationship with the instrument. If, for example, you are trying to develop more small-muscle finger action, or the use of more arm weight, or a more flexible wrist, you can devote your full attention to making such adjustments, sensing how they feel and listening for differences in sound.

You can also focus on listening to various musical aspects of the scales or arpeggios themselves, as well as experimenting with different physical approaches that facilitate playing. Focus on perfecting evenness, for example. Listen intently to the duration of each note and how each relates to the other rhythmically. Then listen to the intensity of each note, trying to match how loud or soft the notes are. Experiment with using the wrists and arms to compensate for differences in finger strength. Observe and optimize the use of the wrists and forearm, as well as the position of the elbow. Note the role of the upper arm and torso as you move up and down the keyboard, experimenting with moving less or more, as well as a variety of distances between the torso and the keyboard.

Practice scales and arpeggios incorporating small degrees of accentuation in groups of two, three, four, five, or six. Learn how much accentuation vitalizes the material without going over the edge into "lumpiness." The use of accentuation has become a neglected art, and yet it was of great importance to nineteenth-century musicians. American pianist William Mason (1829–1908) traveled to Germany to study with Liszt. Mason returned home and wrote a book that claimed to present Liszt's technical method. The book presented accentuation in various groups as a fundamental skill. Liszt endorsed the book, thanking Mason for having put into writing these important basic principles.

An important aspect of all music-making is tempo control. You can sensitize yourself to degrees of tempo by practicing scales at different speeds. Work with a metronome, increasing the speed of the material by small increments. As you do, note the change of focus in listening, more rapid playing inviting perception of notes in larger groups of notes. As you approach your top comfort zone, experiment with adjusting component parts of the body, especially fingers and arms.

Once again, experiment with torso flexibility. Try moving the torso to allow the wrists and arms to remain in one line as much as possible as you move up and down the keyboard. Engage the back, letting it move between positions of uprightness (when you are at keyboard center) and being somewhat curved (at keyboard extremes).

As you adjust the metronome to greater speeds, differences in articulation and texture will also take place. Never sacrifice accuracy or the sensation of being in control. When you sense you are approaching your maximum speed, stop. Then, still using the metronome, take the speed back down by small increments, sensing how to slow the tempo, an important part of the exercise that is often overlooked.

Involvement in this type of work will nourish a spirit of challenge and exhilaration, generating the same kind of "must-do" attitude that drives people to climb mountains or strive for Olympic gold. Remind yourself often that such work is not an end in itself, but rather provides you with the best means possible to achieve you musical goals. Just as a craftsman takes pleasure in having the best possible tools with which to work, you should take pride in building a reputation for having a killer technique.

Plan a long-term program to develop all the skills listed and set aside a segment of time to work on that program each day. Be careful, however, not to push yourself beyond the limits of your concentration or your physical stamina. Practicing such material is apt to get dull despite your best creative efforts. Moreover, backing off when you begin to feel fatigue is a habit you must form if you are to avoid physical damage.

In planning your technical regimen, you should also include material designed by other musicians, much of it purporting to have at least some musical value. When deciding where to turn, you should first decide whether or not to devote time to the vast literature of studies that are designed to develop technique, but cannot be used as performance material.

The early nineteenth century produced a library of this type of material, one that has been supplemented by every generation of composer-pianists since. In this category we think immediately of Carl Czerny's prolific output. Not far behind these exercises or exercise-like pieces are works by Brahms, Burgmüller, Clementi, Cramer, Dohnányi, Gurlitt, Hanon, Heller, and Moszkowski, to mention only a few of the better-known ones. Whether or not to make use of this material is a matter of individual assessment, constitution, and purpose.

Finger exercises are the least interesting in this category. These range from exercises for stretching and independence, such as those of Brahms and Dohnányi to those based on repeated patterns of notes, such as Hanon. Musical attractiveness varies. Most musicians would deem the Brahms finger exercises more interesting than those of Dohnányi. Finger exercises have been around for a long time, some for more than a century, because pianists or teachers in every generation have deemed them useful. Still, as with all exercise, boredom may set in quickly.

Some finger exercises address finger independence. These may seem difficult at first, but once coordination and independence are established, the skills do not usually erode. Thus, after a certain point, practicing these exercises every day is probably not the best use of your time. One might compare mastering such coordination skills to gaining coordination of motor skills like typing or driving an automobile. Once you achieve a certain level of proficiency, you know how.

Other finger exercises are designed to stretch the small muscles or tendons. These must be used very cautiously, for they can lead to both soreness and inflammation. When you use them, you should proceed gently and in moderation, paying close attention to sensing physical limits. Many pianists like to use this type of exercise as a daily warmup, comparable to work at the barre by dancers or vocalizing by singers. If you adopt this pattern, sense when you are warmed up and movement is fluid. At this point the exercises have served their purpose. Do not continue to use them with the vague notion that they are "good for you," because they are both potentially dangerous and not the best use of your time.

Exercises of repeated patterns, such as the famous set by Charles Hanon (1819–1900), may be useful if you incorporate other goals when you practice them. For beginners whose fingers are not yet under control, they can provide repetitious material that frees the mind to focus on the desired coordination. For more advanced pianists, they can serve to acquire other skills. Hanon's suggestion of transposing the patterns to keys that require combinations of white keys and black keys is useful, for this activity leads to learning how to play comfortably in the area of the keyboard close to the fallboard. Developing this comfort carries over into the literature, where more complex passagework often demands using combinations of black and white keys.

If you are trying to adjust the roles of various playing units, playing repeated patterns frees the mind to focus on the desired adjustments. Examples were mentioned earlier, such as feeling more or less involvement of the small muscles of the fingers, or more or less arm weight. Predicable patterns allow the mind to concentrate on sensing physical processes. But as with the finger independence and stretching exercises, use of this material should be limited to the amount of time you can concentrate on your desired goal. In the original publication of his exercises, Hanon suggested playing through the entire book once every day, stating that it only takes about an hour to do so. He observes that this is a small investment of time considering the promised results. His comment reflects nineteenth-century perceptions of time and discipline. Today most of us would neither agree with nor follow his recommendation!

At a higher level of interest than finger or repeated-pattern exercises are the exercise-like pieces that are designed to develop some technical skill, but do not typically appear in the performance repertoire because they are musically impoverished. Here, too, degrees of interest vary. Some might regard Hanon as stultifying but playing Czerny as interesting enough to be worthwhile. Some might find Cramer inspired enough to be musically rewarding, but Czerny to be arid.

Some collections contain both types. Clementi published his *Gradus ad Parnassum* near the end of his career (1817), mixing less-interesting pieces designed to introduce a technique with more musical pieces that represent an application of the technique. Stephen Heller (1813–1888) wrote many sets of pieces designed to develop technique. These are of good musical quality, but only moderately challenging for those who want to develop advanced skills. This entire body of material is fascinating to explore, but how much of it is useful on a regular basis is very much a matter of individual taste. Given the vast concert repertoire available to pianists, such exercise-oriented pieces probably represent short excursions for most pianists rather than main-line development.

Indeed, some might bypass all this material in favor of moving directly to etudes that can be programmed, trying to bridge the gap by starting with the more accessible ones. The usual route is to move directly to the Chopin etudes, for they enjoy the reputation of being among the most challenging technically and satisfying musically. Before you start on the Chopin, however, you might look at such etudes as those of Moritz Moszkowki (1854–1925) or Edward MacDowell (1860–1908). Their technical demands are not quite as extreme, and they are worthwhile musically, often even fun.

When approaching the Chopin sets, choose the first few wisely. Your teacher should be able to offer suggestions. Several are brilliant and hard enough without being at the upper end of the virtuoso spectrum. The "Black Key" (Op. 10, no. 5) "Revolutionary" (Op. 10, no. 12), "Aeolian Harp" (Op. 25, no. 1), "Bees" (Op. 25, no. 2), "Butterfly" (Op. 25, no. 9), and "Ocean" (Op. 25, no. 12) are generally considered good etudes to begin with. Hand extension is often at the heart of Chopin's writing, so remember to heed signs of fatigue or strain. Some of the most attractive Chopin etudes are also some of the most treacherous. Do not fall into the trap of allowing too little time to master the endurance challenges posed by Op. 10, no. 2 (for the fourth and fifth fingers of the R.H.), Op. 25, nos. 5 (double thirds), 6 (double sixths), 10 (octaves), or the famous 11 "Winter

Wind." These may be etudes to work on, but they often require an extra measure of time after they are learned to become fluent and secure without tiring.

The Liszt etudes differ from those of Chopin in that they usually touch upon a variety of technical problems within a single piece. Some of the more popular ones are also some of the most accessible: "La Leggierezza" ("Lightness"), "Un Sospiro" ("A Sigh"), "Waldesrauschen" ("Forest Murmurs"), and "Gnomenreigen" ("Dance of the Gnomes") are good examples. Others offer more challenges, but their drama makes them unusually attractive. Some examples from the Transcendental Etudes (S.139) are number 8 ("The Wild Hunt") and number 10, as well as number 3 ("La Campanella") from the Paganini Etudes (S.141).

In both the Chopin and Liszt sets, do not overlook the value of more lyrical etudes, both technically and musically. There is much to be gained by learning the Op. 10, no. 3 or 6 or the Op. 25, no. 7 of Chopin, as well as "Paysage" ("Landscape") or "Harmonies du Soir" ("Harmonies of the Evening") from the Transcendental Etudes of Liszt. Two wonderful, lyrical mini-etudes open a set of three Chopin wrote for a method put together in 1840 by Ignaz Moscheles (1794–1870) and François-Joseph Fétis (1787–1871).

The fascination with writing pieces designed to address pianists' technical development has flourished throughout the twentieth century as well. Debussy's set of twelve etudes, dedicated to Chopin, explores many of the same technical challenges, such as double thirds and sixths, as well as octaves. Debussy added more challenges by writing and titling etudes for chromatic passages, ornaments, repeated notes, arpeggios, and chords.

Scriabin's early set of twelve etudes, Op. 8 (1894), is modeled after those of Chopin, but the etudes incorporate Scriabin's penchant for intense emotionalism. Later sets of eight, Op. 42 (1903), and three, Op. 65 (1912), represent Scriabin's stylistic evolution. All, however, are rooted strongly in hand extension, some to an extent that they may be impractical for pianists with small hands.

Rachmaninoff has contributed seventeen pieces, which he designates *Etudes-tableaux*, Opp. 33 (1911) and 39 (1916–1917). These "picture etudes" are akin to those of Liszt in that they tend to address a variety of technical problems within each piece. These etudes represent Rachmaninoff's mature style, musically and technically challenging because of their unusually rich sonorities and complex textures. They also often reflect the fact that the composer was endowed with unusually large hands, so managing their challenges with a more typical hand size often requires special attention, such as redistributing notes between the hands and rolling or splitting large chords.

Early twentieth-century etudes by major composers include sets of four by Igor Stravinsky, Op. 7 (1908); nine by Karol Szymanowski, Op. 4 (1902); four by Sergey Prokofiev, Op. 2 (1909); and three by Béla Bartók, Op. 18 (1918). Olivier Messiaen also wrote a set of four etudes focused on rhythm (1949–1950). The first and fourth were influenced by the cultures of Papua and New Guinea, and the middle two represent tight serial organization. Charles Ives wrote several etudes, many of them unfinished. The two best known are a slow one entitled "The Anti-Abolitionist Riots" (1908) and a L.H. one humorously called "Some Southpaw Pitching" (1909).

The late twentieth century is represented by the eighteen etudes in three books (1985–2001) of György Ligeti. Some of these reflect the composer's interest in Afro-Caribbean rhythms. One of the most popular carries the fetching title "The Devil's Staircase." Paul Creston wrote more than a hundred etude-like pieces in ten volumes entitled *Rhythmicon* (1977). Other significant sets are by American composers William Bolcolm, whose set of twelve won a Pulitzer Prize in 1988, and John Corigliano, who wrote five etudes into a continuous set he entitled "Etudes Fantasy" (1976).

Those interested in etudes based on jazz styles should explore sets of short etudes and compositions by the Canadian jazz icon Oscar Peterson, probably written in the 1990s and published in 2005. Nikolai Kapustin is a prolific composer of jazz-like piano pieces and has turned his attention to writing etudes in his Opp. 40 (1984), 67 (1992), and 68 (1992).

You should remember that concert etudes are, indeed, still etudes: studies designed to address technical problems. Despite the bonus of their being musically interesting to both performer and audiences, you should not overlook their purpose. Therefore, set aside time to focus directly on mastering whatever technique is inherent in the work. Doing so in the context of the expressive aspects of the piece should make the technical work easier and more exciting, but it still has to be done.

Some musicians embrace the concept of eschewing work on technical development separately from the repertoire itself, usually with the belief that one can use passages in the repertoire as tools with which to develop technique. Arguments for this view emphasize an economical use of time and avoiding literature that is not first-rate. Several caveats attend it also, however. First, the music we play from the standard repertoire was created for its own musical goals. Its technical demands are sporadic and do not necessarily cover the gamut of skills that constitute a virtuoso technique. One could, for example, play a large amount of repertoire without addressing the development of a virtuoso octave technique.

Second, the musical goals of the piece are usually served better if one comes to the work with a substantial amount of the technique in place. This principle is obvious to us when we deal with beginning piano study, for we develop hand position and reasonable control of the fingers before we undertake pieces. If there is too much to encompass when learning a piece, trying to incorporate so many different goals at the same time may work against developing an integrated musical performance. One can, indeed, grow through meeting technical challenges of hard pieces, but before they are undertaken, some measure of technical prowess should be in place.

Third, technique in pieces should always be studied in the context of the musical demands of the work, for *how* one solves technical problems is dependent upon *what* one wants to hear. Full focus on the physical processes may not even be possible without taking musical concepts into consideration. Nor is it even desirable, for ignoring such concepts in order to practice technique will very likely result in acquiring facility that only partially supports the musical goal you want.

As noted earlier, practicing technique by itself allows you to focus completely on the physical process, thus shortening the time needed to perfect that process. You can and should, moreover, add your own menu of musical demands. Playing scales with a high degree of articulation mezzo forte, often useful in repertoire of the classical period, demands a different type of finger technique from playing scales piano with as little articulation as possible, as might be needed in impressionist music. You can and should learn how to do both, as well as a host of other touch types, and setting up a technical regimen to acquire these skills turns out to be the most efficient and complete approach.

6

Exploring Skills

It is easy to imagine the following. A singer picks up a guitar and improvises a song to honor a dinner guest. A dancer at a children's party creates movements that suggest elephants, eagles, or dolphins, to the delight of all. A minister is asked to give an invocation at a social gathering and offers a prayer on the spot. A newsperson must broadcast a "breaking news" bulletin, reading at sight. What if you were asked to meet equivalent challenges? Could you do it?

If your answer is "Sure I could," then you are on the right track toward placing your music-making in the context of a larger audience and building your reputation as a musician. If you answer, "I haven't practiced today," or "I'm not a very good reader," or "I really don't improvise," then you need to make some changes. If you can't sit down and play *something*, read a piece of sheet music, or improvise a rousing "Happy Birthday" or "S/he's a Jolly Good Fellow" to support a spontaneous celebration, you are compromising your image as a musician.

Granted, these examples do not represent the highest moments of the art you practice, or represent you in your most brilliant light. Even so, they challenge you to be a complete musician, not merely a performer of classical repertoire. That repertoire is marvelous and sustaining for those who love it, but it appeals to a limited audience. Most of the people you contact through daily activities will not, in fact, share your love of the music that is so important in your life. Most will, however, respect your passion and achievement. By the same token, since they are not part of your inner circle, they will have only a partial understanding of the artistic goals to which you aspire and the discipline required to achieve them. Rather, they will simply regard you as a musician . . . a piano player . . . and they assume you can pound out golden oldies, provide music for easy listening, including some of your own stuff, and read well enough to support grandma's rendition of "Over the Rainbow."

These expectations are often attended by a casual acceptance of conditions that for you can range from merely annoying to nearly "impossible." You may be greeted with cavalier comments like "We know the piano is out of tune, but we'll enjoy the music anyhow," or "We don't care if you make a few mistakes and we probably won't even notice them," or "Can you play something we can dance to?"

Remember that you do not have to be everything to everybody when dealing with this issue. But you need to have developed at least some skills to a workable level, both to interact with those around you at these times and to deepen your own musicianship. The fact that you can improvise in some easy-listening style or play something you wrote does not qualify you as a great composer. But it can provide occasions of enjoyable music-making for both you and your listeners. The fact that you can play or read through a few favorite sing-along songs does not make you an expert collaborator-arranger, but it will contribute to your reputation and respect as a musician.

Exhortations to develop these skills may not be enough to get you started. Many musicians who pursue artistic goals find they feel uncomfortable putting their music-making in casual or less than desirable environments. You might understandably ask how you can work for precision, nuance, and expressive intensity for hours every day, and then throw these goals to the winds to accommodate those around you in a social situation. Such questioning might lead you to resist developing these skills. This reluctance might even seem valid until we remember some of the musicians who had fantastic reputations as improvisers. Bach, Mozart, Beethoven, and Liszt come to mind immediately. In fact, for the past two and half centuries, improvising, reading fluently, transposing, and playing by ear were fundamental to being a highly trained musician. Acquiring these skills was an integral part of becoming an artist, not a supplement or an adjunct to such achievement.

Was such a perception right, or is it a superfluous relic of the past? Let's answer that question by looking at what learning to improvise does for us. In order to be able to improvise, you must develop a strong sense of inner hearing, so that you have an aural image of the musical idea a split second before it actually takes place. This is the same inner-hearing skill that serves us in the performance of our repertoire. It is the skill that keeps our flow going in the face of performance pressure, keeps our mind focused so that memory lapses do not occur, and allows us to submerge ourselves in the expressive intensity of the music (see chapter 8).

Moreover, improvisation demands conceptual organization of the music, a flow that moves from short motives to phrases, to sections, to overall planning of a piece. It requires knowing what elements logically follow one another, thinking of rhythmic motives, harmonic progressions, and arranging them in understandable patterns. It stimulates conceptualizing and projecting the emotional content of the music, creating an interplay of dynamics, articulation, and technical display.

The carryover should be obvious: that learning to conceptualize and execute music while improvising trains us to perceive and project the repertoire we choose to play. Indeed, every musician who has learned to improvise testifies that doing so sharpened insights into the music of other composers. Improvisation stimulates greater awareness of the basic elements of the music as it unfolds, which in turn leads to greater security in performing all repertoire.

Improvisation may also lead to composition. History reports that Mozart improvised his first six sonatas (K.279–K.284), playing them on tour before he wrote them down. Such a report suggests that as one improvises, some ideas, some patterns are so pleasing that one wants to capture them by repeating and refining them, You may repeat some version of them in your next improvisation session. Gradually details may become set, so that improvisations become pieces you play, but ones that are not written down or recorded. Writing them down or recording them is the next step. At this point the music tends to solidify to the point of becoming compositions other musicians may want to play.

Many examples of such crossovers may be cited. The early sonatas of Mozart were just mentioned. The recordings of many famous jazz pianists, such as Art Tatum, Oscar Peterson, or Bill Evans, have been transcribed into musical notation and are available, and some pianists find them worthwhile to study as repertoire material. Similarly, Vladimir Horowitz was famous for his playing of a medley of themes from Bizet's opera *Carmen* and his rendition of John Philip Sousa's "Stars and Stripes Forever." Although it is reported that Horowitz never played these show pieces quite the same way twice, his recorded performances of them on a given occasion have been transcribed into musical notation, and pianists are learning and programming them.

What about learning to read fluently? This skill is the gateway to exploring the treasure house of literature that is available. Once you learn to read well enough to perceive what the composer is trying to say in a given musical composition, you are able to add hours of enjoyment to your musical life and enhance your knowledge of the literature. Some pieces you read will be the equivalent of a magazine article, enjoyable for a short period of time, but quickly set aside. Other music you will want to earmark for possible inclusion in your repertory at a later time. Some music will excite you so much that you will want to start working on it as soon as possible. But the upshot is that reading and exploring will become a habit, one that you are likely to enjoy on a regular basis.

Learning to read also leads to collaboration with other musicians, one of the most enjoyable and rewarding aspects of your profession. The spectrum of collaboration is broad, from sight-reading extemporaneously to support a singer or instrumentalist, to exploring, rehearsing, and presenting in concert selections from the inspired song and chamber repertoire.

Moreover, your insights into music and performance will almost always be broadened and strengthened by working with others who love music, as you do. They may approach music differently, find different values, deal with different technical issues, but knowing how other musicians think, learn, and play results in deepening your own understanding and strength as a musician.

Three specialized skills should be noted: transposition, open score reduction, and realization of figured bass. The ability to transpose at sight is desirable if you wish to work in the field of collaboration, particularly if you work with singers. Its fluency depends on being able to both read and analyze on the wing, much like an improviser would. A second skill is that of reading and reducing a score for multiple players at sight. If you wish to work in the field of accompanying choral groups or rehearsing theater productions, such as opera, you need to be able to extract the musical ideas, arrange them for keyboard, and play them, all as part of an ongoing process.

The third skill, realization of figured bass, figures prominently in history, for it was an integral part of the prevailing style in the late Baroque and early classical periods. All keyboard players were expected to be fluent in its practice. Thus, they were able to provide a harmonic foundation for groups of performers, read symbols that denoted harmonies, and "realize" them by moving smoothly through the indicated progressions, fleshing out chords and adding melodic passing tones, passage work, and ornamental decoration.

This practice all but died out in the nineteenth century as composers chose to write for the piano with greater specificity, thus eschewing performer improvisation. A reincarnation of the practice took place, however, in the twentieth century in the context of traditional jazz, although the harmonies were more complex and the symbols for them somewhat different. Being able to realize chord symbols remains a useful tool for today's pianists, particularly those whose interest includes playing jazz.

All of these more specialized skills are desirable in that they strengthen overall musicianship. Each prepares you for specific types of work. Most pianists garner some degree of facility in one or more of them through their college-level training. However, many stop short of developing them to a professional level unless they seek to work in the indicated fields, or they find themselves in a situation in which they are needed on a regular basis.

Let us return to focusing on the two skills every pianist should develop, whatever their professional goals: reading and improvisation. Having stated a rationale for taking time away from performance preparation to develop these skills, the fact remains that, in most cases, you must assume the responsibility for maintaining an ongoing program to develop these skills. Most teachers will encourage such development but won't have enough time in piano lessons for more than sporadic or cursory examination of what you are doing. Thus, you might want to consider taking lessons or classes designed to develop these skills specifically. If seeking out such instruction seems too time-consuming or expensive, don't panic, because a lot of your development can take place with your effort alone.

Let's look at reading first. There is only one way to learn to read fluently: devoting time to reading on a regular basis. Thus, set aside time for reading every day in your practice schedule. There are two kinds of reading that can take place: reading in order to get acquainted with the music itself, and reading that focuses specifically on fluency and accuracy. In the former, we may "read through" a difficult piece that we want to get to know, possibly for consideration for our personal repertoire. This reading may be sketchy in places, halting at times, sometimes correcting as you go along in order to get the sense of the music. Often the music is difficult, beyond your ability to read fluently.

This kind of reading is useful, and your ability to psych out a composition will improve as you practice. You strive to be as fluent and accurate as possible, of course, but your purpose is to grasp the style and dimensions of the music at hand, so you may read sketchily. This type of reading should, however, be combined with the other area mentioned: reading for fluency and accuracy.

The key to improvement in this area is to choose music that is easy for you. If you are a poor reader, start with beginning-level piano pieces. Whatever your fluency, select a level of difficulty that is low enough for you to be able to read it rhythmically, without breaking down, and with a high degree of accuracy. Doing this will not only train you to be fluent but also will ease your possible discomfort for sight-reading, eventually building your confidence. Spend some time finding materials at the right comfort level for you, eventually moving to a more advanced level, but never moving up so rapidly that you sacrifice fluency and a high degree of accuracy. There are several things to remember when you undertake this reading:

- Identify key and time signature.
- Look at the music before you try to play it; try to hear it as clearly as possible.
- Keep the pulse strong and moving; play as slowly as you have to; count if necessary.
- Keep the eye moving slightly ahead of the actual music to see what's coming up.
- Learn to find new hand positions without looking at the keyboard.

The last skill may require extra work for those whose development as a pianist is strongly rooted in glancing at the keyboard frequently to assist the hands in moving about. Such work might consist of creating simple exercises in which the hands learn to change positions at various intervals, learning to skip a third, fourth, fifth, or octave without visual assistance, and finding such intervals in various keys so that both white and black keys are involved.

An example of such an exercise would be to start by playing a major triad on middle C in the right hand. With your eyes looking away from the keyboard (i.e., toward an imaginary score on the music rack), move the hand and play a D-flat major triad. Move back to the C major triad. Now move to a D major triad. Then move back to C major, to E-flat major, back to C, E major, back to C, F major, back to C, and on up the keyboard, using triads in half steps. Try to focus and sense distance as you do this exercise. At first keep chord roots within an octave range. You are likely to make some mistakes. Try to correct them by readjusting your sense of distance without looking at the keyboard.

When this exercise begins to go well, move on to other types of triads, minor, first and second inversions in both major and minor, seventh chords and their inversions. Eventually try it with open octaves, starting with small intervals and moving out over an octave. Then begin the process with scalar passage work, playing major and all versions of minor scales without looking at the keyboard. Start with scales with a range of one octave, and eventually move to two and three octaves.

The same series can be applied to the left hand. also. The L.H. needs to develop an additional specialized skill, one that reflects a frequently encountered accompaniment pattern. This pattern consists of playing a single note or octave in the low register of the keyboard, then moving the hand up toward the middle register and playing a chord. This "om-pah-pah" pattern is ubiquitous in keyboard music.

For most people, practicing this skipping pattern in reverse is easier to coordinate. So play the first inversion of the C major chord with the L.H. thumb on middle C, if possible using the fourth finger on the lowermost note, so that the little finger remains free. Then move down the scale stepwise, playing single notes with the little finger, alternating between the chord and the single note played by the little finger. Once again, proceed slowly, trying to sense distance. Gradually incorporate black keys as well as white.

As you get more secure, expand the exercise to include other types of chords in the middle range, increasing the distance the hand and arm have to travel, eventually incorporating octaves as the lower component. As the arm has to travel longer distances, avoid reaching out from the elbow. Incorporating the upper arm in the to-and-fro motion will lead to more secure guidance and greater accuracy. Be sure to keep the back and torso flexible as you play the chords in the middle range, sitting far enough away from the keyboard to minimize twisting of the hand at the wrist.

Remember the key to success in developing sight-reading is consistent practice. You can also give your reading skills a boost by setting aside a certain period of time to concentrate more heavily on them. For example, you might focus on reading with special emphasis over the period of a summer, amassing appropriate materials and working every day for thirty or forty minutes.

There is yet another advantage to becoming a good reader, for once you develop your reading fluency, you can use it to earn extra money throughout your career. Many opportunities to collaborate with individuals or groups will present themselves, starting with your student years, and becoming a good reader will allow you to take advantage of them.

Now let's consider how you get yourself to start improvising. Many pianists who have been trained traditionally find they are hesitant to "make up stuff." Part of this reluctance comes from the fact that they have developed their pianism to the point of being able to study masterworks, and what they produce when they try to improvise is neither focused nor inspired. They conclude, in fact, that what they make up sounds dumb, so they eschew further attempts.

Thus, it is useful to start thinking about improvisation by just playing around without attempting to organize what you do into anything, just making sounds. Identify them in some way, so that you can remember and organize them if you decide you want to. This is the equivalent of a general physical warmup exercise in which you simply swing your arms, bend your knees, move your head around, twist your torso, and so on. Here are some things to do:

CHORD WARMUPS

- Play the tonic chord in any key up and down the piano with both hands. Use all positions. Do this in all major and minor keys. Use both triads and filled octaves. Use both block chords and broken chords (some kind of arpeggio).
- Play a series of major chords (both hands), moving up chromatically, then by whole steps. Do this with minor chords; now alternate major and minor; do this with first-inversion chords, then second-inversion chords.

- Do all the preceding exercises with chords to which you add a minor seventh from the root (like a dominant seventh chord in major).
- Do all the preceding exercises with chords to which you add a major seventh from the root (as in C, E, G, B for major keys or C, E-flat, G, B in minor keys).
- Do all the preceding exercises with chords to which you add ninths or thirteenths. You can also think of these notes as added seconds or sixths of the scale (in C these notes would be D and A). If you have been playing the same notes in both hands up to this point, adding these extra notes will probably require you to begin splitting a single chord between two hands, such as C, E, G, and B in the L.H. and D and A in the R.H.

This introduces new possibilities, so you can try splitting the chord in various ways, as well as doubling one or more of the notes somewhere, or leaving out one of the notes somewhere (often the fifth of the key). Such dispositions of chord tones are often referred to as "voicing" by improvisers. Begin to take note of which combinations you think sound "cool."

Begin to combine chords from different keys, trying to keep track of the good ones. Try, for example, combining any two keys a whole step apart (C and D, F and G, etc.). Mix triads and seventh chords in various ways. You will begin to see that some of the combinations end up being the same as or similar to sonorities you have already discovered. (For example, combining C major with a major seventh with D minor could also be viewed as having added the ninth, eleventh, and thirteenth of C.)

PASSAGE WORK WARMUPS

You probably play basic scales already, so let's start by playing scale combinations, such as C major in the L.H. and D major in the R.H. Try all possible combinations. Then try these combinations using quarter notes in one hand and eighth notes in the other; reverse hands; notice what implied sonorities you pass through. Expand by using ratios of three to one or four to one.

Begin to work with patterns that double back, such as playing three notes up and dropping back one note for the second set (C, D, E—D, E, F—E, F, G, etc.); apply to both hands first, then only one hand with the other playing a basic scale; reverse hands. Now create a pattern with four notes rising, dropping back one, going through all the versions indicated. Branch out to other keys. Combine different keys.

By this time you know how to invent combinations of various patterns you already know, having realized that the variety can go on and on. Hopefully you will have tried enough combinations and patterns so that you feel free to romp around the keyboard, creating sonorities and bits of passage work. You are, in fact, improvising. Perhaps not in the style you would like, with the level of organization or sophistication you would like, but, still, you are making up stuff at the keyboard. You should continue to improve playing these sonorities and patterns as you add the next challenge, for such free exercises develop both recognition of keyboard patterns and combinations as well as the facility to play them.

The next challenge introduces the idea of improvising with themes or motives. At this point you will begin to play with a pulse. Keep the rhythmic patterns short also. You might start by setting your name to a musical motive. If you have a name of several syllables, use only your first name; if your first name has only one syllable, add your middle or last name. Observe the kind of phrase that seems to result and form it into a rhythmic motive. For example, "David" or "Mary" results in a long-to-short pattern with stress at the beginning, like a two-note slur. "Elizabeth" or "Fernando" suggests upbeats. Ask yourself whether your setting fits with a duple or triple count and if what you have created suggests a major or minor mode. Play the motive at various levels with various harmonies, repeating it in the R.H. with some kind of sonority in the L.H. Begin to count a pulse with it and move it about. Finally, change or prolong one or more syllables of your name so that the underlying pulse is changed (if it was duple, change it to triple, and vice versa).

Now take your motive and keep it within a single pitch-frame while beginning to move the L.H. harmony around. Use nontraditional procedures, such as parallel major chords with added minor sevenths. Keep one of your pulses. Add complications by breaking up the L.H. chords in some way. If you don't know what to do, start with simple arpeggios or an Alberti-like bass pattern.

Keeping a pulse, play your motive in very long notes, beginning to move it around, while the L.H. uses shorter note patterns. Reverse the idea by playing your motive all over in more rapidly moving notes, while the L.H. has more sustained patterns.

If you have followed these ideas thus far, you are aware of the fact that the gate to improvisation has been opened for you, that the possibilities are limitless, and that you are making up music as you go along. If you protest that a motive is not a composition yet, then add another motive, or extend the first one with a similar one that is related to the first in some way, either by creating a question-and-answer relationship, extending it, or fragmenting it.

It is important also to remember that improvisation exists in all styles. You may be conditioned by today's society to link improvisation only with popular styles, such as jazz, gospel, or New Age. As a result, you may feel like your own improvisations are somehow disappointing because they don't sound like a contemporary style you admire. Just remind yourself that musicians improvised long before the advent of today's popular styles. If you want to incorporate a contemporary style into your improvisation, whether it is jazz, New Age, gospel, or rock, you can do so once you are ready to take on more complex challenges.

That being the case, you should still begin by learning your way around the keyboard and, once you garner some degree of freedom, begin to select whatever appeals to you within the framework of these exercises. If you are targeting a specific style, spend time listening to professionals who play in that style. As your knowledge of basic materials increases, what you build up in your mind through listening will coalesce with your newfound facility. You will begin to identify certain gestures as belonging to the type of music you want to play. Identify these gestures and perfect them. Enhance these gestures by continuing to listen and analyze what the practitioners of that style do. Consistent alternation of listening and analyzing, along with the incorporation of characteristic hallmarks, will mold your own improvisation style in the direction you seek.

A few closing observations may serve to keep you on track:

- Remember that thinking in nontraditional patterns keeps you from sounding too mundane. So don't be afraid to experiment, to try combinations. If you don't like what you hear, you don't have to go there again; if you do like what you hear, remember it so you can go there again.
- Try always to hear inwardly any and all combinations, even the wild ones before you play them. Your projected hearing may not be perfect at first, but it will improve, and you will develop the ability to pre-hear many of your favorite combinations in any key.
- Incorporate a rhythmic/pulse element, and, before you close out any improvisation session, try to sustain an uninterrupted rhythmic flow for a given amount of time. If this is hard for you, keep it going for half a minute at first, then increase the time.
- Work constantly at developing keyboard facility in response to your mental signals through the free warmup technique. Constantly challenge yourself to something you haven't tried before, increasing the challenges. Facility depends on your hands and fingers developing enough coordination to be able to respond to your creative mental signals. As you conceive various patterns, particularly those typical of R.H. passage work, you may find that you have to slow the tempo to play them, just as you would in learning a new piece of written music. So be prepared to gain security playing complex patterns by applying the techniques you use in traditional music.

Be patient with yourself. Remember that becoming a fine improviser takes just as much time and effort as becoming a fine performer of traditional classical repertoire.

7
—

Developing Performance Chops

At some point you should consider how well you like to perform, for performing is an integral part of a musician's life. You are a musician, so you have chosen not only to work in this art form but also to share its wonders with those around you. When you undertake this communication, you want to represent the music in its most glorious form. Your audiences will range from people who find listening to you pleasurable, but who know little about the intricacies of music, to other musicians, whether they be peers or professionals, who know every detail of what you are doing. Performances may be of little consequence for your goals, or may be of great importance. Whatever the circumstances, a performance is a performance, and you will want to present yourself in the best possible light. You need to assess your degree of comfort as you approach the intense psychological state generated by performance, and, if you are like most people, you will need to train yourself to handle some degree of stress.

A few people simply love the idea of performing. Just as there are "natural" athletes, so there are "natural" performers. These individuals relish whatever tension they feel before a performance and are vitalized and empowered during a performance. Often these folks performed during childhood with an innocence that did not recognize any particular consequence attending performance. They simply did what they were prepared to do, and often enjoyed adult approval and admiration as a result. Once conditioned in this way, they are able to incorporate and pursue professional goals, even after they become aware of the stakes involved. Thus they are able to rise to important performances with a minimum of psychological duress.

Most people deal with a greater degree of discomfort when considering the demands of performance, one determined by various factors, such as what is at stake, degree of preparation, that it takes place at a specified time, physical condition, and, sometimes, environment. If you identify with this majority, just accept that dealing with the stress of performance is part of the gig, that almost everyone has to face it, and that you can learn to handle it successfully. Others have done it, and so can you. Think of all the professionals who face some potentially stressful "performance," situations in which they must focus to order to carry out what they were trained to do.

The list is long. Obviously musicians, dancers, and actors perform. Lawyers perform when they appear in court; doctors perform when they operate; ministers and teachers perform when they speak to an assembly. Businesspeople perform at board meetings, to effect sales, to conduct interviews. Law enforcement, military, and firefighting personnel perform in the line of duty. Technicians, pilots, and vehicle drivers perform. Performance is involved whenever anyone is challenged to exercise skills at the optimum level and/or to achieve predetermined goals.

You thus realize that many professional activities generate performance stress. So exorcise the temptation to dramatize your performance challenges. Like almost everyone else, you will have easy performances, tough performances, smashing performances, and a few you don't like. Regard performance as something you take in stride as a part of your profession.

Train yourself to prepare meticulously, both musically and psychologically, and learn to trust your work and talent to bear fruit when performance time arrives.

Preparing yourself and trusting yourself, however, involves more than just telling yourself these are attitudes you want to adopt. In fact, getting yourself to the psychological state where you feel prepared and trusting is a long-term project and involves as much long-term preparation as learning to play your music. You expect to practice your repertoire every day, coming to it with an attitude of dedication and willingness to work. So it is with getting yourself ready to handle performance pressure.

How do you do that? First, you must introduce yourself to your own psyche. Who is this person that lives within your body? Is this a positive, cheerful person who expects the best from every situation? Or is this a person who expects to be singled out for nasty surprises by fate . . . or luck . . . or the odds . . . or whatever you call it? If you are like most people, you are neither one totally, but a combination of both, being positive and upbeat sometimes but also buying into a "life sucks" attitude at other times.

So start by examining your thought patterns to see how much counterproductive thinking you are doing. This includes all those seemingly benign thoughts that are, nevertheless, based on the premise that the universe has singled you out for special malevolence. How often we apply this type of negative thinking to everyday activities! No matter how fleeting or insignificant these perceptions seem, they still do damage. Here are a few examples:

- Why do I always get in the line that doesn't move?
- Why does this traffic signal always turn red when I am in a hurry?
- Why does the weather always turn bad when I plan something out of doors?
- They'll probably sell out before I get there.
- Good guys finish last.
- I must look terrible.
- With my luck, . . . (fill in some worst-case scenario).

Yes, in fact, these circumstances might befall you, or these perceptions might be true. But they also might *not*. So you do yourself harm by assuming your destiny is to be shortchanged. Gradually a negative self-image takes shape, and your subconscious is taught that your fate is to be victimized. And in the bargain you construct the barriers that undermine achieving your personal best when you are under pressure.

Sometimes we confuse humility with negativity. Thus we deflect compliments because somehow we think it is the attractive thing to do. "That was a wonderful performance" is countered with "Oh no! It really wasn't that good." "I loved your Chopin" is answered with "But my Mozart wasn't so good, was it?" Often we even contradict our admirers by exaggerating flaws or focusing on details we believe could have been better. Thus, "Congratulations on a wonderful recital" is answered with "But I had a problem in the Bach." A more balanced approach is to accept the positive and think about what could be improved later.

Perhaps the most damaging pattern is predicting performance shortfall. A students sits down to play at a lesson and announces, "This isn't going to be good," or "I can't play this piece," to excuse the fact that the piece is still being learned. Early performances in classes or for friends are prefaced with "This will probably fall apart," or "I know I'm going to forget in some places." Yes, there may be elements of truth in these statements because the music is new, but if you are testing your ability to perform a piece, you should establish the habit of expecting to succeed rather than falter.

As musicians we sometimes regard our efforts negatively because of how we perceive the achievements of peers. A well-known saying illustrates this prevalent pattern: "Everyone sounds so wonderful through the practice room door." This statement reflects the feeling of inadequacy many experience when they compare themselves to their peers, but also implies that our perceptions are not always accurate. In reality, everyone must work hard to achieve. Everyone must face and overcome problems. Everyone must fight against performance anxiety.

Maintaining a perspective that does not denigrate your talent and achievement requires constant vigilance. Doing so is absolutely necessary, however, if you are to build a deeply rooted concept of your own value and ability. Moreover, you need to convince yourself that all of this positive preparation will, indeed, work in your behalf. You must buy into the theory that positive perception of yourself will trigger your subconscious to impel you toward success during performance, no matter how much anxiety your conscious mind might be experiencing.

Psychologists continue to study the complex relationships that exist between the conscious and subconscious levels of the mind. They do not agree on the role of the subconscious, but one theory views it as a powerful force for determining how we respond to external stimuli. If it is "fed" attitudes by the conscious mind consistently, it will eventually accept them and use its power to direct our final decisive actions, no matter what the momentary state of the conscious mind.

Acting upon this theory, we should prepare the subconscious by consistently selecting thoughts that support the outcome we desire with our conscious mind. It does not matter if some level of the conscious mind does not accept achieving such goals as inevitable. Go through the motions, calling up thoughts that assume successful outcomes. Once the subconscious accepts what the conscious mind is insisting, the result will be assured. Philosophers have echoed this belief through the ages, including Jesus Christ's "As a man thinketh, so is he" and Buddha's "What we think, we become."

It is easy to dismiss this line of thinking as feel-good pop psychology, especially in our technology-oriented age. Still, it is inevitable that we adopt some attitude toward performance. So we can either cast ourselves as a victim trying to cope or as fighter trying to conquer. Assuming you prefer the latter, realize that the fighter prepares by training over a long period of time, building strength, and focusing on winning.

The challenge, then, should be to program yourself in favor of positive expectations. You need to work constantly to reject every negative or insecure thought pattern that crosses your mind and substitute a positive, goal-oriented thought instead. *How dumb*, you think. It's okay if that thought crosses your mind. But do it anyway.

Think of all the things we do as pianists that could be considered dumb. Finger exercises are dumb. Scales are dumb. Hanon is dumb. True enough, if you evaluate these activities only by their potential for moving or thrilling an audience. But think of them another way. If you work on them consistently, bringing to them as much attention and intelligence as you can, they can be useful tools with which to build finger strength and independence, learn patterns you will encounter in pieces, and develop a fluent, flexible technique. They are tools you use to achieve more important goals.

Controlling the mind is not that much different. Practicing seemingly dumb mental patterns builds psychological strength, teaching the mind patterns of confident thinking and conditioning it to be flexible and agile during times of stress. Accept the theory that the conscious mind has the power to choose thoughts, constructive or destructive, and influence the subconscious. The subconscious itself does not have this choice, but its power lies in impelling you toward bottom-line results by directing your automatic response system. It is the agent that will direct and inspire you when the conscious mind is flying around the room trying to deal with anxiety and pressure. But this powerful entity must be *fed*. It must be nourished over a long period of time, so that it comes to believe implicitly that success is your goal. When it accepts that belief, then it has the strength to make it a reality, no matter how agitated the conscious mind becomes or how you think you feel.

Daily practice of those dumb positive thoughts is the food with which to nourish the subconscious. Every time a negative though crosses your mind, reject it and feed the subconscious a positive thought. The positive thought need not deny reality, but give every thought a positive spin. If some part of the conscious mind doesn't quite believe the substitute thought, it doesn't matter. The subconscious mind will be nourished whether or not the conscious mind believes. The conscious mind's job is simply to make the positive choice consistently. Then, when the pressure is on, the subconscious will do its job.

Here are examples of negative thinking shown in Table 7.1. Some may have a familiar ring.

Even if you think this line of thinking is foolish, try it anyway. What have you got to lose? Indeed, you will probably find that keeping positive thoughts going consistently is a challenge in itself. You'll be able to substitute a positive thought for a negative one for a period of time, but then

Table 7.1.

Negative Thought	Substitute Thought
"I'll never be able to play this passage!"	"If I am patient, I will nail this passage."
"My teacher will hate this performance."	"My teacher will have valuable ideas for me."
"He plays this piece much better than I can."	"His performance inspires me to achieve."
"So-and-so doesn't like my playing."	"I know I can move so-and-so with my playing."
"I always get so nervous."	"My excitement will enhance my performance."
"What if I forget?"	"I know this music so well, it will flow effortlessly."
"I don't know how to practice."	"I continue to organize my practice time better."
"I don't have enough technique."	"My technique is getting stronger all the time."
"I don't have a feel for this music."	"I am understanding and responding to this music."
"What if I fail the audition!"	"I will do my best; the rest will take care of itself."
"My performance was so bad."	"Much was good, the bad shows what to improve."
"There is so much competition out there."	"It's exciting to be in a vital, creative environment."

something is likely to happen that will completely wreck your attempts to be upbeat.

Examples abound. Your teacher will ask to hear something in a lesson you hadn't planned on playing. You play it, but afterward feel like you were not able to show your best work. You must play on an unfamiliar piano, and you are not comfortable with its response, so you feel like your attention was given over to dealing with the instrument, not to making music. You worked very hard on a passage yesterday and felt you made progress, but today it seems no better, so you are frustrated and negative.

At such times you experience a negativism that is emotionally charged. That emotional power tends to feed on itself, exaggerating whatever happened into a prediction for all time. The discomfort you experienced at that lesson grows into "I never play well for my teacher" or "My teacher probably thinks I am untalented." The experience with the recalcitrant piano is transformed into "I will never be able to handle a strange piano" or "I just don't perform well in public." Your frustration over not having achieved your practice goal becomes "I will never be able to play this piece" or "I will never have enough technique" or "Something is basically wrong with me."

It is precisely at these moments when you must refuse to accept downgrading yourself. It is often not easy to turn your mind away from dwelling on your disappointment. Remember that turning away does not mean simply trying to avoid thinking in such patterns, but rather substituting something positive to take the place of the negative thought. Okay, but that's *dumb*! Yes, but we've addressed such sentiment already.

So just do it. If you practice this psychological routine day in and day out, you will get results. No, nervousness will not be eradicated altogether, but some part of you will be stable and calm enough to see you through to doing your best. And that is what you hope for, after all.

Insisting upon this mindset is the most difficult when anxiety begins to kick in just before a performance. People experience a variety of sensations when they are about to perform. Some reactions are shortness of breath, extreme fatigue, physical weakness or loss of control, upset stomach, inability to focus, and mental withdrawal. This is precisely the moment when you must fight back.

Every time you begin to worry about who is in the audience, that hard page, that tricky passage, the piano, not forgetting, or whatever, force your mind back to some positive thought. Pay no attention if some part of you feels this process is ineffective. Do it anyway.

Here are a few examples of positive thoughts. Use them as a springboard to create your own:

- I love this music, and it is exciting to share it with people.
- I have paid my dues and am prepared to play this music.

- My excitement gives me untapped creativity.
- I have planned for this performance, and I am going to enjoy every moment.
- My mind is clear, and my body is in tip-top shape.
- I relish this experience.
- I feel inspired.

Return to these thoughts or similar ones again and again. Just before a performance, combine them with activity, both mental and physical. Move out of your shell. Practice deep breathing, stretch your back, swing your arms, take an interest in the details around you, crack a joke, drink some water, talk to the person backstage about the weather. Leave time just before you step out onstage to listen to the music inwardly, focusing on the sounds you want to produce.

As you face your audience, heed the advice that the aforementioned teacher, Olga Samaroff, gave her students: "Remember that ninety per cent of your audience will be predisposed toward liking you or not between the time you walk on stage and the time you play your first note." So greet your audience with a countenance that suggests your greatest pleasure is to be there to play for them.

After the performance, do not permit the normal release of tension to turn into a feeling of disappointment with the performance itself. The let-down can invite you to give a negative spin to what you have just done. Accept whatever congratulatory gestures are offered. Remember that the performance is not over until your audience has gone home, so graciously receiving those who want to compliment you is part of the gig. During this time of decompression, discipline your thinking to avoid reruns of what you think you did.

After the excitement of the performance has cooled and you are able to keep private counsel, you can evaluate what you did. Keep in mind that you cannot be completely objective about the performance because you were the performer. One cannot both fly the plane and sit back as a passenger. Even so, you should take stock of the performance at some point, for doing so is an important part of your development as a musician.

No performance is perfect, so there will be details you believe could have been better. These will probably tend to surface first as you consider what you did. For every instance of weakness, create a plan for strengthening or correcting it. Do not simply stop with mentally wringing your hands and wishing somehow that you could redo this or that. Rather, detail how you will work to improve.

As you evaluate, try to give as much thought to what went well as what was not up to your expectation. Dismissing the good summarily may tip the balance toward the negative, and your goal is to form an honest impression of your efforts. Even the details that you deem satisfactory can be improved, so as you consider the good things, think what you will do to enhance their attributes and make them even better the next time.

You will repeat the cycle of preparing, anticipating, performing, and evaluating throughout your career as a musician. It is a dynamic, ever-changing process. It might be compared to surfing. Just as no two waves are the same, no two performances will be the same. Each experience is an adventure, and although its outcome can never be completely certain, you can develop the skill to face each set of challenges effectively. There will be some spills, for no one can respond perfectly all the time. But there will also be exhilarating moments of incomparable reward.

Eventually you and those around your will come to know that being a performer is who you are. No, you can never escape completely dealing with the challenge, even the anxiety, of performing, but with persistence and practice you will learn to relish its excitement and manage its demands.

Using Your Mind

There are important mental techniques you should work on as you grow musically. These develop gradually much the same way as your piano technique and musical understanding, requiring that you conceptualize goals and practice on a regular basis. Although they might seem ancillary to your main goal of learning piano music, they are vital to your overall development as a musician. Regard them in the same light as the automatic body functions that support healthy living, such as breathing or coordinating eye and hand movements. Let's consider concentration and several types of listening.

CONCENTRATION

Concentration is a state of mind in which your full, undivided attention is focused on a single activity. It is somewhat like falling asleep in that when you are doing it effectively, you are unaware that you are doing it. Also, just as there are levels of sleep, there are levels of concentration,

You might ask why we need to practice learning to concentrate inasmuch as we do it every day in a variety of tasks. The answer becomes apparent when we consider the environment in which we live. Concentration has always been subject to disturbing distractions. In today's world, the number of distractions has multiplied many times.

Consider, for example, that a century ago the ways you could spend your leisure time were severely limited when compared with those of today. You might have conversed with friends, read a book, played games with family, or worked at some craft, like woodcarving or sewing. Now, of course, choices are extensive, and the variety is staggering. You can watch something offered by dozens of sources, available on TV, online, or in theaters. You can play games, choosing from a menu that ranges from team and individual sports to hundreds of video games. You can pursue a hobby or craft with immediate instruction offered through technology for virtually any interest, from cooking to house building. You can express yourself creatively with technology that allows you to blog, publish, record, and distribute. You can socialize. Wow! How you can socialize! Online networks allow you to stay in contact with literally hundreds of old and new friends around the world.

What a terrific age we live in! The attractions are so great that we can, and often do, partake of many different pleasures. And since there are so many, we learn to move from one to the other quickly, shifting our attention in rapid succession. Moreover, we learn to divide our attention effectively, so that we can carry on a conversation and tweet at the same time, or watch a movie and talk to someone on the cell phone at the same time. Thus we train our minds to jump around rapidly and to juggle, and after a while, the excitement of jumping around and juggling becomes addictive.

Having the flexibility to change focus rapidly or to multitask is not all bad. These too are developed skills and can often provide stimulating variety and sometimes useful efficiency in dealing with the superficial details of daily life. But kaleidoscopic mental activity does not mix well with some other of life's activities. One example is reading that demands comprehension on more than a superficial level. So if you read great literature, poetry, or legal documents, you need to be able to concentrate. Another is any kind of devotional activity: meditation, prayer, or worship. If you are to reap benefits from such efforts, you must focus. Also, studying to comprehend complex ideas or memorizing information requires sustained concentration.

As you may have guessed, performing music, even listening to music intelligently, is one of the activities for which you need to concentrate. Performing or listening demands that you simultaneously conceptualize what you hear, relate musical ideas to what has happened or is going to happen, synthesize the experience with abstract concepts, and process emotional reactions. If you are performing the music, the process is further complicated in that you produce the music itself through your physical, intellectual, and emotional responses.

Yes, there are times when deep involvement does not take place, just as there are times when you scan what you read or pay marginal attention to what is on TV. As a music listener, being only partly attentive is often without consequence. As a performer, however, creating music without full concentration courts insecurity and poor communication.

Thus, you need to focus intensely when you work seriously at the keyboard. Begin by scheduling piano practice at a time when you will not be interrupted. Let your friends know that you do not answer your cell phone or text messages during practice time. Most people in your life would not expect to pull you away from a school classroom during a scheduled class time unless it was an emergency. Encourage your family and friends to regard your practice time with the same respect.

If you are interrupted (and you surely will be occasionally), don't be grumpy about it. Rather, try not to react emotionally, for such a reaction disturbs your psyche and makes returning to work harder. Deal with the interruption as efficiently as possible and then return to your practicing.

Sometimes you may start your practicing with a scattered or worried state of mind. Other times it may be difficult to settle down for no apparent reason. If you are worried about something important, you may not be able to concentrate deeply on your work, just as you might not sleep well. But often, not being able to concentrate immediately is a side effect of leading a busy life.

When this is the case, you need to be both patient and persistent. Stimulate focus by creating something different from your usual routine. For example, listen for something new in your warmup exercises rather than running through the same pattern. Often working on new music demands enough attention to invite focus. Similarly, when you practice music you already know, engage your mind by being creative. Experiment with a new way of shaping a phrase, moving toward a climax, or timing a ritardando. If you are working on technique, avoid repeating passages while your mind is thinking of something else, for such drilling doesn't do much good and invites bad habits. You might even injure yourself. You wouldn't hang -glide or skydive without paying attention to what you are doing. Then, don't practice octaves or double notes without close attention to physical processes and your degree of fatigue.

If you achieve only partial concentration and fear your practice time is inefficient, don't let yourself off the hook completely. Continue to try to engage your mind. Watch the clock if you must, but discipline yourself to work the planned amount of time. Establishing a pattern of dropping into effective concentration easily will likely take several days of consistent work, just as, for example, it takes days of physical exercise to see or feel its benefits in your body. Be patient and persistent, and effective concentration will develop.

You can also establish patterns away from the piano that contribute to the effectiveness of your focus. Learn to manage a busy life without reveling in its pressures. Rather than insisting on repeating to everyone how hectic your life is or finding satisfaction in the self-image of being busy, busy, busy, choose to deal with life's demands with as little fuss as possible.

As you do so, enlist humor whenever you can, for it often helps relieve tension. Imagine what a funny story your frustrations will make at a later time. Frequently remind yourself that dealing with mundane matters without fuss results in having more time at the piano with the music you love. Reflect on how much you love *your* time and the pleasure it gives you. Regarding your work at the piano as something wonderful will pave the way for effective concentration when at last you can turn to it.

LISTENING

Listening is an aspect of concentration that has special connotations for musicians. It means more than just processing what you hear on a superficial level, and it takes on different meanings when examined in various contexts. Musicians incorporate several types: listening to yourself, listening collaboratively, listening across the repertoire, and inner-listening.

LISTENING TO YOURSELF

When you are extremely attentive to the music you are producing, we say you are "listening to yourself." If your reaction to what you hear is positive, you reinforce what you are doing. If your reaction is negative, you make changes. Although this listening process seems obvious, it does not always take place efficiently. Making sounds at the keyboard does not necessarily mean you are listening carefully enough to perceive accurately what you are doing. Some musicians work with recording devices at various stages of preparation, believing they can evaluate their music more precisely when they are not involved in creating it.

Listening is especially challenging when we often repeat small segments of music, such as in the early stages of learning a piece, or later trying to secure the notes in our fingers, or later still trying to work them up to speed. Repetition tends to bore the mind, and attention to the music wanes. A dichotomy develops between what the fingers are doing and where the mind is. Soon this separation becomes both comfortable and usual. Nourishing this state is very dangerous, for it leads to both uncommunicative playing and insecurity in performance. The instant pressure enters the picture, your mind will realize it has not engaged in the playing process and will gravitate to negative, fearful thoughts. The result is feeling out of control during performance.

Obviously, then, you should avoid this trap in your practicing. Many techniques to keep the mind attentive are traditional. The most frequently encountered suggestion is to inject variety into what you are playing. Change rhythms, dynamics, or speed as you repeat passages, for doing so throws the mind off balance enough to keep it involved. Another is grouping the notes into patterns that are more easily perceived or executed, such as practicing playing as a group the notes that move in the same direction in passage work. Practicing hands separately is another. This procedure is often used when the notes are first being learned, but unfortunately is often abandoned after the hands have been put together. Revisiting it regularly not only engages the mind but oftentimes reveals weaknesses.

Even when we pay attention to what we are doing, we cannot focus on everything at once. As you practice, you should turn your attention to various aspects of the music. Listen for dynamic control and nuance at one point, evenness in passagework the next, then tempo consistency, phrasing and articulation, balance between the hands, and pedaling. Paying attention to each of these in turn both engages your mind and refines your musicianship.

Learning to listen carefully to what you are doing is a never-ending quest. The good news is, however, that immersion in careful listening generates greater perception and understanding of the music itself. This leads to increased sensitivity to the emotional content of the music and the freedom to project it.

LISTENING COLLABORATIVELY

When you play with other musicians, you need to listen in a somewhat different way, for you incorporate into your perception not only what you are doing musically, but also what your collaborators are doing, synthesizing these components into a coordinated whole. Thus, your focus on your own music-making must extend outward. Such reaching out is often reflected in your posture and where you look.

Observe ensemble playing the next time you attend a professional concert where the pianist is a collaborator. You will probably identify body language that shows the players are attentive to one another, effecting balance, rhythmic precision, and expressive projection. If the collaboration is a piano concerto, where the soloist is out front next to the orchestral conductor, you will be able to sense and possibly see the communication between the soloist and the conductor. Experienced pianists also know that visually seeking out or nodding toward an orchestra instrumentalist who has a solo passage encourages both the soloist and collaboration.

This kind of multifocus listening needs to be practiced. Pianists who are not used to shifting attention outside the immediate sphere of the keyboard often find doing so initially distracting, even generating insecurity. The first step is to seek many opportunities to collaborate. Find a musical partner you enjoy working with and plan to make music together on a regular basis. As you prepare for rehearsals, imagine the presence of your collaborator, and practice glancing up and away from the keyboard and your score. Identify places in the score where fleeting visual communication will be helpful to the ensemble, such as at tempo changes or cadences.

In collaborations between two musicians or in small ensembles, balance must be addressed. Sometimes the pianist is, indeed, an accompanist, for the piano part merely supports the musical ideas played by your collaborator(s). In most collaborative literature, however, the pianist is a musical partner with solos, countermelodies, and moments of brilliance. Thus expert collaboration becomes more complex than supporting others and staying in the background. Balance challenges often result in an ongoing discussion with your collaborators.

When you prepare a piano concerto, it is very important to learn the entire score. Learn and memorize orchestral interludes just as you do your own part. Practice the orchestral accompaniments to your part. If the orchestra has the melody or even a melodic component, learn to sing it while you play your own part. And finally study the instrumentation of the orchestral part, using a recording to train your ears and adjust your texture to blend effectively with that of the orchestra. Be aware of where and how much to project your sound so that the orchestra does not cover you.

You realize by now that playing collaboratively demands that you prepare your own part securely to focus on many issues outside your own sphere. In early eras the keyboard instrument was often regarded as the stable center in collaboration, providing the harmonic framework. The piano's role has become more varied and sophisticated, but psychologically it still remains a fundamental component in those works that incorporate it. Thus the responsibility the pianist must take on is significant.

Recognize that the pianist often has a more complex part in collaborations, if for no other reason than that the piano score is typically more than a single line of music, unlike the parts of most other musicians. Thus pianists frequently need to spend time preparing their parts before collaborative rehearsals begin. When you agree to collaborate, be prepared to commit a segment of your practice time to the project.

Not all musicians understand the complexities of a piano score, so others sometimes assume you can read your part as easily as they read theirs. For pianists who are good readers, sight-reading collaboratively is surely possible, but only up to a point. The accompaniment patterns that are typical of early vocal music are sight-readable, but the piano part of many art songs by nineteenth- or twentieth-century composers much less so. The challenges of chamber music, too, are often greater. A few pianists might be comfortable reading masterworks by composers of the classical period, but fewer will be able to read those of later composers. For most pianists, even good readers, it is best to avoid having to read complex piano scores in ensemble rehearsals. Rather, insist that you be allotted time to prepare your part, so that everyone concerned is happy with what you are able to bring to the collaboration.

LISTENING ACROSS THE REPERTOIRE

Music is the focus of your professional life, so obviously you need to spend time listening to the performances of others. The music you will probably seek out first is piano music, perhaps performances of music you are studying or are planning to study. Opinions differ as to how much to listen to the repertoire you are working on. Some fear you might be too strongly influenced by performance(s) you hear, thus compromising your exploration and personal interpretation. Indeed, powerful performances leave strong impressions that can influence easily. Thus some would advise you to limit listening to professional performances of the music you are studying until after you have learned and shaped the music yourself. Others endorse the opposite extreme and would urge you to listen to as many performances as possible, note differences, remember what you liked, and mold your own performance accordingly.

There is no clear answer as to which method is best. If you study performances, choose your models carefully. Today's technology allows dissemination of the good, the bad, and the mediocre. Even if you listen only to fine performances, be careful not to buy into any performance to the extent that you begin to copy it without doing your own thinking. Remember that any performance is just *one performance*. Great artists often present quite different interpretations of the same literature. Many artists recorded the same literature more than once during their career because they felt differently about the music at different points in their lives. Thus even the most attractive performance cannot be regarded as definitive. You need to listen, learn as much as you can, and then work to develop your own relationship with the music.

Whether you listen by downloading, playing recorded music, or going to live concerts, you should incorporate listening to some music that is *not* centered around the piano. There is a vast literature of chamber music without piano, both for strings and wind combinations. There is also the wonderful world of vocal music, extending from art songs to opera. The orchestral and choral repertoires are vast and colorful. Expanding your horizons through listening broadens your perception of the piano music you add to your repertoire. For example, to absorb the energy you need to bring to the keyboard music of J. S. Bach, listen to the Brandenburg Concertos. If you want to shape beautiful lines in your Mozart, listen to his operas. If you want to incorporate the heroic grandeur of Beethoven into your performances of his sonatas, listen to the symphonies. If you want to understand the intense intimacy inherent in your Schumann piano pieces, listen to his lieder. The crossovers may not take place immediately, but when they do, your understanding of style will increase and ultimately benefit your performances.

INNER HEARING

Now let's consider the kind of listening that is perhaps the most fundamental to your musical development. This listening is sometimes called "inner hearing." It exists in all of us to some degree. If you stop and think of music that is very familiar, you can run through the music in your mind. Just pause and think of a popular song, a national anthem, or a folk melody you learned as a child. You find you can run the entire piece through in your mind. This is especially easy if words are involved. The same process is active when you complain that you can't get a tune out of your head. Advertisers engage this faculty by repeating short snippets of music, jingles that stick in people's minds and are linked with products.

This faculty is of vital importance to musicians. Properly used, it is the prime mover of all music-making. This cycle should start with hearing the music inwardly, this mental impulse triggering the physical response that follows. This process becomes more difficult as the music grows in complexity. Engendering inner hearing for a folk song or a commercial jingle is one thing. Doing so for a complex score that represents a composer's ingenuity and emotional palette is much more difficult.

Moreover, when we recreate the music of composers, another entire mental process is involved, that of being able to hear the music you see on the printed page. As with other facets of musical talent, the natural ability to hear what you see on the page varies with each individual. Just as a few people are gifted with the ability to identify any pitch by letter name (called "absolute pitch" by musicians), so some are able to hear what they see with a high degree of accuracy. For most, however, the ability to hear what you see is less than perfect. It will also vary with the type of music being read. Older music based on traditional harmony, melody, and rhythm is usually perceived in more detail than music based on more contemporary techniques. For many, inner hearing of nontonal music will be quite sketchy.

This ability should be strengthened both for the naturally gifted and for those whose inner hearing is weak. Singing is considered the most natural way of expressing the music we hear inwardly. Thus most music training includes sight-singing classes that offer opportunities to practice inner hearing by singing what is on the written page.

There are several other ways this process can be enhanced. For pianists, looking at the score away from the piano and hearing as much as you can is a good exercise. If you are just beginning to develop this capacity or if the music is complex, you may not be able to hear with a high degree of accuracy or in great detail. Sometimes you will be able to discern only rhythmic patterns or the contour of a melodic line. Do not give up. Rather, continue to work to bring together what you see and what you hear. Try to hear as much as possible, and then fill in what you don't hear by playing here and there. Then return to looking and try to hear more inwardly. If details become vague, play again. Then look again, alternating the two activities until clarity improves.

Practicing away from the piano should be continued after you have learned to play a piece. Instead of actually playing it, place the score in front of you and simulate the process of playing by triggering all the neural impulses. Some people like to do this and move the fingers and arms on a desk, on your lap, or in the air. Others simply feel the neural impulses, but don't really move the muscles at all. In both cases, the process is triggered by the inner hearing that takes place as you read the music. A more challenging version of this is "playing" the music after it is memorized. In this case, you do not look at the score, but simply hear the score inwardly supplemented by the various images the trigger your memory, once again "running" the piece without actually playing it.

Yet another technique for strengthening inner hearing is "playing by ear." This means simply trying to play accurately music that you already hear inwardly. There was a time when this activity was frowned upon, probably because it was assumed that those who played by ear would never learn to read music. This ability sometimes led to approximated performances of well-known classical pieces, offending those who prized recreating the composer's intentions accurately.

Playing by ear need not, however, be used to maul classical literature, but rather to develop inner hearing and in the bargain a useful skill for social situations. As noted in chapter 5, a pianist is rightfully embarrassed over not being able to play "Happy Birthday" or "For He's a Jolly Good Fellow" because of not having the skill to produce an accurate, rousing performance by ear. Yet sadly, many pianists who can play Beethoven or Chopin beautifully are unable to meet this challenge.

Try to set aside some time regularly to play by ear. Pick out melodies. Figure out harmony, even if you have to do so by trial and error. Try different dispositions on the keyboard until you develop your own style of fleshing out the basics into an attractive arrangement. Develop your repertoire of social standards, such as those mentioned, as well as some holiday songs everyone knows and even a few standards drawn from the vast repertoire of pop tunes. This activity should supplement the free improvisation skills discussed in chapter 5. One might even regard it as a practical application of the ability to improvise, so the two activities should quickly coalesce and enhance each other.

Finally, inner hearing should be the genesis of all performance. Before you press a single key to produce any sound at the piano, inner hearing should take place. That hearing, in turn, triggers the physical response to play what you hear. Clear inner hearing will, moreover, prompt your physical response to make whatever adjustments are necessary to produce the sound you focus on inwardly. Then as you play, you listen to what you have produced, evaluating it in terms of the inner hearing. Thus a cycle is set up: inner impulse triggers playing that in turn triggers evaluation. Meanwhile, new inner-hearing impulses have taken place. This continuing cycle propels you as you progress through your performance. It gives focus to your concentration, ensures continuity, and helps prevent breakdowns.

This description might suggest a cycle that is complex and awkward. How can we be sending new impulses to our playing mechanism and evaluating what has just been done at the same time? We do this all the time—every time we open our mouths to speak! Consider that before we start talking, we have formed a concept of what we want to say in our mind. As a result of that concept, we speak, using our physical skills to form the words, put them into sentences, and vocalize them. At the same time, we are aware of whether or not we actually said what we wanted to say. If once in a while a word comes out wrong, we laugh and correct it. In a conversation, this process goes on in a continuous cycle without our being self-conscious about it. As musicians we need to achieve similar fluency in a cycle that starts with inner hearing.

For many highly trained pianists the inner-hearing side of the cycle is weak. Some have not thought about its importance. Many never take the time to strengthen it. They overlook the primary impulse because they focus so intently on following the markings in the score, meeting the technical challenges of the piece, and trying to evaluate what they play. The cycle is thus incomplete. The result is that often they fear losing continuity.

Thus working to strengthen the inner-hearing side of the cycle should be a constant activity. You should take the time to study the score without playing it. You can also practice hearing a score inwardly at various points during the day. When you encounter having to wait for something, as we all do every day, rather than fuming impatiently, turn your attention to music you are working on and hear it in your mind, even if it is just a passage.

And above all, every time you sit down at the piano to start a piece, be sure you begin by taking a few minutes to listen to what you are about to play. Set the mood, the tempo, even simulating the first physical impulses with which you will begin. Never press a key until you have heard inwardly the sound you want to create. You thus set up the cycle in the right order.

The development and active use of inner hearing cannot be overemphasized. If you need to work to strengthen this area, it is of utmost importance that you undertake exercises to get the job done. Progress may be rapid for some, slower for others. But be persistent, for a strong sense of inner hearing is at the heart of all secure musical performance.

9

Creating Fantasy

A well-known teacher was conducting a master class. A student had just performed the first movement of a Mozart piano sonata. The performance was well prepared technically and musically, but it had not engaged the audience. The teacher began the lesson by walking up to the performer, still seated at the piano, pointing to a place in the score, and asking, "What do you want the audience to feel here?"

Surprised by the question, the student answered, "It's marked forte there."

The teacher responded, "Yes, I see the marking, but forte tells you to play loudly. It is not a feeling."

Perplexed, the student tried again, "Well, it is at an important cadence."

The teacher smiled, but said, "A cadence is a harmonic progression. It is not a feeling."

"The chords are marked with accents."

"I know, but accents are indications of touch, not feelings."

Frustrated now, the student cried out, "Well, I guess I don't know."

The teacher nodded, turned to the audience, and stated what was obviously the punch line of this inquiry, "Well, if *you* don't know what you want the audience to feel, how do you expect *them* to know!"

One might accuse this teacher of using contrived dialogue at the expense of the student. Teachers sometimes employ such techniques to drive home a point. The lesson here, of course, was that although the student had prepared efficiently and performed well, the final step of communicating the essence of the music to the audience had not been realized.

Most would agree that music should reflect feeling and express an emotional state. Most people listen to music to experience that feeling in some measure. They may tap their feet, nod their heads, move their torsos, or sit quietly, but, as they listen, they immerse themselves in feeling joyful, sad, wistful, heroic, inspired, desolate, giddy, or any number of other emotions. The raison d'être of music is, in fact, that it can reflect and project all shades of human emotion, whether or not they can be described with words.

Our challenge as musicians is to discern the emotional essence of the music we perform and communicate it with enough intensity to bring our listeners into the sphere we create. Ideally, for the duration of our performance, those who listen are transported out of the reality of their existence and partake of the realm we create. This union may be imperfect, varying in intensity, or sporadic, but it must be forged to some extent if our performance is to achieve its purpose.

It thus becomes apparent that we must learn to discern the emotional qualities within the music we study, relate them to our personal emotional experiences, and project them to our listeners. To some extent, responding to the emotions of the music is inherent in our love for music. As musicians we already have a head start, because we were drawn to our profession by this very power. It is easy for musicians to become sidetracked, however, because we turn our attention so often and so intently to the processes of preparing ourselves to perform. We feel the need to develop our technique, study the composer's intentions, relate to teachers' suggestions, deal with unfamiliar instruments or venues, and manage performance anxiety. Amid our efforts, however, we should remind ourselves often that these challenges only lead up to the most important goal, that of effectively expressing the emotional content of the music.

But don't assume you can simply turn on an inner switch to be expressive after you have learned a piece. Identifying and highlighting this emotional content requires thought, patience, and practice. Achieving emotional projection is an ongoing, complex process, bound by several strong, intertwined influences.

First, recognize that you have a personal level of comfort when dealing with emotional expression. Some people find emotional display easy, others less so. Moreover, our society encourages emotional control in most situations. We may get mad, but cultivate anger management as an attribute. We curtail expressions of romantic feelings, because we are afraid of being too obvious in the game of love, or worse, we fear rejection. We find refuge in privacy during times of sickness or mourning. As children we are taught to be quiet, respectful, and demure in public places.

Such control seems sensible because much of the time we live in places of population density, often with limited space, so keeping a low emotional profile is practical and courteous. However, such cultural expectations foster personal discipline, resulting in reluctance to let go emotionally, even in the context of artistic expression. Thus projection of the emotions in the music we want to share may be mitigated to the point of rendering it mild at best and ineffectual at worst. Often we observe teachers urging students to play more incisively, increase dynamic contrasts, or throw themselves more deeply into the mood of the music.

Yes, there are a few who are naturally over the top. If you are one of these, you may be cautioned to tone down the emotionalism in your music, refine your expression, play more steadily, or pay more attention to the directions in the score. Recognizing where you stand naturally on the spectrum of emotional projection reveals your starting point and the direction you will need to take.

Second, you know already that music varies considerably as to the appropriate degree and type of emotional projection. Part of this variety comes from the period in which the music was created, part from the temperament of the composer, part from a performance tradition that evolved over generations. Examples abound. You do not approach the music of J. S. Bach with the same mindset as that of Claude Debussy. The periods in which these men wrote music were reflections of different societies and philosophies. You do not play Mozart with the same concept of texture as you play Beethoven. Although both are regarded as composers of the classical period, their personalities were quite different. When you begin to study a piece by Chopin, you study performances of others to help you achieve subtle values the score does not indicate, such as tempo metamorphosis, rubato, and bel canto.

Third, your own immediate environment may shape the degree and type of your emotional projection. You may find yourself performing on large, small, good, or bad pianos, in venues that range from parlors to amphitheaters, for audiences whose makeup varies from being children to seniors. These factors are more subtle than the first two, but they still have some influence on the degree and type of emotional expression that is possible or desirable in any given performance.

Recognition of these influential parameters is helpful, but you still need to forge a detailed recipe to determine the degree to which you need to stoke your own fire and project your emotional responses. Here are some steps you can and should follow.

Start with the usual research, but as you work, combine research with a degree of imagination to recreate the environment of the music. What philosophical, political, social, or economic conditions were prevalent at the time the music was created? What were concepts of time like? How did people dress? What did their furniture look like? What did they read? How did they spend their leisure time? How long did it take to travel from place to place? The Internet facilitates access to a great deal of this information. Historical periods, moreover, are recreated often in film. (But beware! Many are romanticized to some extent.)

That these quick glimpses are so easily available is great, but try to supplement the surfing by dipping in more deeply occasionally. The easiest way to start is by seeking out artworks that inspired the composers who wrote the music we play. Read the literature; visit galleries or access reproductions to absorb the visual art. Sometimes the connections to piano music are specific. Here are some examples shown in Table 9.1.

Specific connections at times describe events, such as Brahms's Edward Ballade: Op. 10 no. 1; Schumann's Carnaval, Op. 9; Liszt's Mephisto Waltz,

Table 9.1.

Composer	Piano Music	Literary Work or Artwork
Schumann	*Papillons*, Op. 2	Jean Paul Richter's novel *Fliegeljahre* (final chapters)
	Kreisleriana, Op. 16	E. T. A. Hoffman's novel *Kater Murr*
	Verrufene Stelle (Haunted Place)	Quotes Hebbel's poetry
Liszt	*Années de pèlerinage*	Based on Goethe's *Wilhelm Meister's Apprenticeship*
	Au lac de Wallenstadt *Orage* *Eglogue* *Les cloches de Genève*	All inspired by lines from Lord Byron's *Childe Harold's Pilgrimage*
	Vallée d'Obermann	Based on Byron and Senancour's novel *Obermann*
	Sposalizio	Rafael's painting *The Marriage of the Virgin*
	Il penseroso	Michelangelo's statue "The Thinker"
	Sonetti del Petrarca	Petrarch's love poetry from the fourteenth century
	Après une lecture de Dante	Hugo's poem reflecting on Dante's writing
Brahms	Edward Ballade, Op. 10, no. 1	Herder's Scottish folk ballade "Edward"
	Sonata Op. 5 (2nd movement)	Quotes Sternau's poetry

continued

Table 9.1. (*continued*)

Composer	Piano Music	Literary Work or Artwork
Musorgsky	Pictures at an Exhibition	Hartmann's artworks (used as titles for pieces)
Debussy	*L'Isle joyeuse*	Watteau's painting *Embarquement pour Cythère*
	Danseuses de Delphes	Architectural friezes in ruins in the city of Delphi
	"Les sons et les parums tournent dans l'air du soir"	A quote from Baudelaire
Ravel	*Jeux d'eau*	Quotes Henri de Régnier's poetry
	Valses nobles et sentimentales No. 1	Quotes Henri de Régnier again
	Gaspard de la Nuit	Poems of Aloysius Bertrand
Rachmaninoff	Prelude Op. 32, no. 10	Böcklin's painting "The Return" (reported by pianist Benno Moiseiwitsch)
Ives	Sonata No. 2 "Concord"	Writings of Emerson, Hawthorne, Alcott, and Thoreau
Griffes	The White Peacock	William Sharp's poetry

Mazeppa, the two St. Francis legends; or Debussy's *La Cathedrale englougie*. At other times the composers identified with concepts or literary connections, sometimes using them as inspirations for nonpiano works or as texts for vocal works. Such influences are more general, but exploring them still offers insights into the genesis of composers' creativity. Here are a few examples shown in Table 9.2.

Even this partial list of ancillary explorations may seem overwhelming. Don't think you have to make these supplemental forays immediately or all at once. But if you create a menu of things you want to explore, returning to it periodically in the context of the music you are studying, you will be surprised at how many areas you can address. As you do, you will be able to identify more intimately with the expressive

Table 9.2.

J. S. Bach	Religious concepts of Martin Luther
W. A. Mozart	Writings of his opera collaborations: Da Ponte, Schikaneder, Metastasio
Beethoven	Writings of Goethe and Schiller
Schubert	Poetry the composer used as song texts: Wilhelm Müller or Heinrich Heine
Chopin	Poetry of Adam Miekiewicz (some believe it inspired the Ballades)
Debussy	Symbolist poets: Verlaine, Baudelaire, or Mallarmé
Scriabin	Philosophy of theosophy, set forth in the writings of Helena Blavatsky
Messiaen	Religious concepts of the Roman Catholic Church

goals of composers. Your own imagination will respond, and your ability to project the expressive essence of the music will become strong and secure.

Many times the piano music you play carries a descriptive title that suggests the expressive tone of the music and stimulates your response to it. These titles range from being fairly specific, such as Schumann's "Child Fallling Asleep" from *Kinderszenen*, Op. 15, to rather general, such as the suggestion of "night music" inherent in the term "nocturne." A few subjects have been favorites of composers, such as water, birds, bells, and nature. Here are a few examples shown in Table 9.3.

When the composer indicates imagery or mood, you can easily follow the suggestion and build on it. The challenge becomes greater when there is no extramusical association, such as in pieces titled prelude, sonata, fugue, or rondo. Should one attempt to add stories or imagery to this music? Not everyone will agree that it is appropriate. Even so, the job remains of lifting your performance above the mundane. You must identify the expressive substance of the music, relate it to personal feelings or experiences, and incorporate it into your performance. Sometimes trying to match emotional events in your own life will trigger responses to the music that will enhance your emotional projection of it. At other times,

Table 9.3.

Rameau	*Le Rappel des oiseaux* (The Chatter of Birds)
Schumann	*Vogel als Prophet* (Prophet Bird)
Liszt	St. Francis of Assisi Preaching to the Birds
	St. Francis of Paola Walking on the Waves
	Nuages gris (Gray Clouds)
	The Cypresses of the Villa d'Este
	The Fountains of the Villa d'Este
Debussy	*Clair de lune* (Moonlight)
	Jardins sous la pluie (Gardens in the Rain)
	Reflects dans l'eau (Reflections on the Water)
	Le Vent dans la pleine (The Wind on the Plain)
	Brouillards (Fog)
	Feuilles mortes (Dead Leaves)
Ravel	*Oiseaux tristes* (Sad Birds)
	Une Barque sur l'océan (A Bark on the Ocean)
	La Vallée des Cloches (Valley of the Bells)
Messiaen	*Catalogue des oiseaux* (13 pieces incorporating 77 bird calls)

just stimulating imagery will help. The following exercises may serve to stimulate your imagination:

- You are a photographer. Imagine this music playing at a gallery showing of your works. What would you have chosen as appropriate visual subjects?
- Similarly, you are a cinematographer. This music is being used to accompany opening scenes of a film. What scenes would you choose?
- Now you are an actor. What role might you be playing for which this music would be appropriate? What setting? What dramatic situation?
- A few years ago, a famous woman pianist built a reputation for changing concert gowns several times between works during

recitals, the dresses reflecting her ideas about the emotional tone of the music. Imagine what clothes you might choose (even if you are male).

- Color is inherent in all of the preceding examples. Now choose a color for each piece, movement, or section of the music you are playing. Use a menu that includes subtle shades, such as lavender, turquoise, beige, crimson, orange, or puce. Add adjectives if you wish, like royal blue, charcoal gray, lemon yellow, firehouse red, or forest green.
- Think now about assigning a surface texture to the music with its characteristic feel. There are many to choose from, such as glass, velvet, wood, sand, cement, metal, cotton, feathers, or tarpaper.
- Rachmaninoff wrote a song (with a piano transcription of the same music) titled "Lilacs." MacDowell wrote "To a Wild Rose." Debussy wrote *Bruyères* (Heather). Schumann wrote *Blumen-stücke* (Flower Pieces). What flowers or plants would you choose for your music?
- Examples of piano music with wildlife references abound: Debussy's "Jimbo's Lullaby" (elephant) and *"Poisson d'or"* (goldfish); Scarlatti's "Cat" fugue and Copland's "The Cat and the Mouse"; an entire set by Villa-Lobos based on animal toys ("The Tin Ox," "The Cotton Bear," " The Glass Wolf"). Can you create your own menagerie in reference to the music are playing?

As you create fantasy, remember that it always has to be tempered by the directions the composer indicated, as well as the style and period of the music. Balancing your own emotional response with these external disciplines is an ongoing, exciting process in itself. The result will be a performance that is truly recreated, one in which you are able to give new life to the expressive ideas of those who created the music, and one that will render your performance both unique and compelling.

10

Securing Memorization

As the eighteenth century drew to a close, the concept of the performer as a soloist rather than a collaborator began to solidify. By the early nineteenth century, an image emerged of the soloist as a consummate virtuoso, revered for extraordinary abilities and even supernatural powers. The Italian violinist Nicolò Paganini (1782–1840) and the Hungarian pianist Franz Liszt (1811–1886) represented the epitome of this concept, both reveling in the public adulation it generated. Liszt wrote in a letter, "Virtuosity is not an outgrowth, but an indispensable element of music."[1]

An offshoot of this evolution was that virtuoso musicians began eschewing sharing programs with other musicians, the usual practice, preferring to give entire programs by themselves. Also around this time they began to include *memorized* performances as yet another way of impressing their audiences. Franz Liszt is often given credit for being the first

---

1. Liszt, Franz. Gesammelte Schriften, iv, Breitkopf und Härtel, Leipzig, 1899.

pianist to memorize solo recitals. Recent research suggests that Clara Wieck Schumann (1819–1896) actually was the first, having given memorized recitals at the age of thirteen at the insistence of her piano teacher, her father, Friedrich Wieck (1781–1873).

The tradition of memorizing is still expected in many types of concert presentations. Solo recitals are expected to be memorized. Exceptions are recitals of new music, music that is extremely complex (some nontonal or serial music), or music in which the score itself plays a role (aleatory music in which the eye randomly selects portions of the score). Pianists generally use music for collaborative performances. An important exception is the standard concerto repertoire, where the soloist is expected to play from memory. Periodically one encounters objections to this tradition or performances in which it is ignored, but it persists despite these occasional efforts to cast it aside.

Is there a reason for memorizing music, aside from trying to impress an audience with your mental prowess? Proponents for memorization point to several attributes. Let's think about them.

First, we tend to remember easily information that is important to recall. Obviously we remember our names, addresses, telephone numbers, email addresses, even, sometimes, personal identification numbers and passwords. We remember landmarks of frequently traveled routes, names of people who attract us, brands of products we use, and all kinds of verbiage that represent things we like, from song lyrics to slogans. Sometimes we remember these things imperfectly, but when we don't have satisfactory recall, we are motivated to concentrate enough to ensure that we remember the next time. Eventually the mental effort succeeds.

We also remember events in our lives, both good and bad, if they are emotionally charged. We recall with pleasure details of our best friend's wedding. We painfully remember the moment we learned of a loved one's death. We remember our graduation day, but also the time we injured ourselves. Like factual details, these things may leave imperfect impressions, but they stick in our minds because they represent details of our lives that for one reason or another were significant.

Now to some extent the process can be reversed. Thus, if you invest time memorizing something, it becomes more important to you, more a part of the fabric of your life, and possibly more meaningful from an emotional standpoint. Of course, this is but partially true if you do not have some degree of affection for whatever it is you memorize. If you are forced to memorize a poem you don't care about, you may recite it one day and put it out of your mind the next. But when you memorize something that is attractive to begin with, you initiate a change in your relationship with the material. You develop a sense of ownership, an intimacy, the feeling that it is part of your emotional palette. Those who advocate memorizing music believe that it fosters a better understanding of the components of the music, an "internalizing" of the music, and eventually a more personal, emotionally involved performance.

This argument is obvious when applied to solo performance. In professional-level collaborations where using the music is traditional, it might be argued that the score is used only as a point of reference, so that the players are free to divide their attention between their own playing, that of the collaborators, and the effect of the entire ensemble. In other words, no one is really performing with their eyes glued to their own score, so to some extent the music is memorized, for it has undergone the study, internalization, and emotional synthesis that memorization presumably supports. The rationale for concerto performance, where memorization is expected, is that the soloist is freed from the score to communicate more effectively with the orchestra, both its conductor and its members at appropriate times.

You see by now that you are expected to be able to play memorized performances for solo performances, competitions, auditions, and most concerto appearances. Thus learning to memorize effectively and play memorized performances securely is an integral part of your professional preparation. You need to embrace it and master it. Here are some suggestions for doing so:

- Memorize constantly.
- Memorize information as you learn.

- Memorize in different ways (aural, visual, geographical/physical).
- Check and drill; break material into components.
- Create improvised versions.
- Rehearse memorized performances.

Let's elaborate on each.

Memorize constantly. You may have heard the often-repeated saying "Memory is like a muscle." The implication is that using memory develops strength, as does using muscles. Practicing this principle means setting aside a segment of time each day to memorize. This is active mental work, more focused than merely testing to see if you can play something without looking at the music. Rather, during this time use the techniques described in the following to study and drill the music at hand. Above all, do not put off memorizing your music until just before performance time. This principle works hand in hand with the next.

Memorize as you learn. When learning to play new music, take the time to concentrate on various aspects of it that will feed the process of playing it from memory. First, break up the music into sections. The score itself will dictate appropriate lengths, but keep the segments relatively small: a phrase or two of a theme rather than an entire statement. Then take the time to hear it inwardly, so the strength and accuracy of your inner hearing are enhanced. As noted in chapter 8, inner hearing acts as the trigger for both remembering and playing the music. Next, observe harmonic progressions, rhythms, patterns for each hand, how the hands coordinate, articulation, dynamics, and pedaling. In short, analyze the music in every way that seems significant. If you take time to do this regularly, you will become so familiar with the components of the music that you will be on the verge of having memorized it. When you do focus directly on memorization, you will have gathered so much information about the music that final memorization will consist of organizing a few details and working for continuity.

Memorize in different ways. As you zero in on the memorization process, consider different kinds of memorization and practice all of them.

Aural memorization has already started with your daily work. Continue to strengthen it by spending time "running" the piece in your head without the music, keeping it at the right tempo, hearing as much detail as possible (dynamics, articulation, sonorities, etc.). As noted, this inner hearing should continue to be the genesis of your music-making.

Other types of memorization act as closely connected supplements, and different people gravitate toward different processes. Some people feel most comfortable visualizing the printed page, a few being so gifted with "photographic memory" that they enjoy almost total recall. Focus on this visualization as one of your memory exercises. Start by visualizing the score away from the piano and simulating playing it in your lap or on a desk. Then, when the visual signals are strong, begin to work small sections at the keyboard.

Many people find focusing on the relationship between the music and the keyboard to be the most effective anchor for memorization. This focus might be termed "geographical" memorization. Using such keyboard imagery does not imply you must constantly look at the keyboard, but only that the process of remembering the music is generated by the imagery of how it is laid out on the keyboard.

This example will help clarify such an approach. If you were directed to play a C major triad on the keyboard, you could do so. How would you remember it? You may have heard the sound in your head, but you probably did not imagine a written example on a page. Rather, something else directed your hand. That "something else" was "geographical" memorization. You knew where the C major triad was on the keyboard; you directed your hand to that pattern of keys and played them.

The great German pianist Walter Gieseking (1895–1956) loved playing a game with the students of his master class. After a day of working, Gieseking and his students often adjourned to a nearby coffeehouse, where Gieseking would start the game by "playing" a piece on a tabletop. Watching his movements closely, the students would vie to see who could identify the piece first. Such recognition was, of course, dependent on recognition of "geographical" imagery.

Observe how easy it is for you to "remember" many processes that involve the whole physique: getting dressed, eating meals, driving automobiles. We "remember" hundreds of patterns in our daily lives because we "know" how to do them. Granted, the patterns used in playing piano music are usually more complex and not repeated as much as those in our daily lives, but the principle is the same.

To strengthen this type of memorization, practice processing the physical movements. Still triggered by inner hearing, simulate playing the music, using fingers, hands, arms, and torso. Larger physical playing units need to be involved as much as possible. Smaller units such as fingers and hands have their role, but guidance from arms, shoulders, and torso complements and supports the process. Focus on images of how the playing relates to the keyboard, thinking about patterns of black and white keys, ranges, movements of playing parts. Then go to the actual keyboard and recreate these images, letting them guide you through the playing.

This type of memorizing is obviously dependent on recall of a physical process, and physical processes have traditionally been deemed unreliable. Indeed, when we are under the pressure of performance, physical processes can be disturbed by the adrenaline in our systems or other distractions. How many times do we hear that we cannot "trust" our fingers when under pressure?

This criticism is valid to some extent, but only when small playing units (such as the fingers) are expected to perform patterns without either mental or whole-body guidance. Fingers are apt to falter when what they are supposed to do has not been supplemented by studying the details of the score, the elements that make up the music, and the way it is laid out on the keyboard.

To some extent the opposite is true. We must prepare memorization in such a way that we are comfortable in letting the physical processes guide us. This confidence relegates self-consciousness to a level that is less likely to disturb the musical flow and allows a measure of freedom for communicating the expressive aspects of the music.

Check and drill. Despite our best preparation, most of us harbor the fear of a lapse in concentration during performance, resulting in a glitch in the musical flow. We are confident that we know the music, but fear that its recall will be momentarily blocked. We have all experienced such moments. We start to introduce someone whose name we know as well as our own, but we can't make the mental connection for the introduction. We start to punch in a telephone number we have called up hundreds of times, but suddenly get the digits turned around.

The traditional antidote to this insecurity is daily memory drill. Although these drills are contrived in that they do not directly support musical goals, they build a subconscious feeling of confidence that helps ward off memory and performance anxiety. The list of such drills is extensive. Here are a few:

- Practice segments, hands separately from memory, simulating but not playing the other hand.
- Practice segments, hands separately from memory, with the other hand inactive.
- Practice segments, hands separately from memory, while singing or vocalizing the other hand. This version can also be used for concertos, where one plays the piano part while singing the main outline of the orchestral part.
- Play three measures; drop back two measures and play three more measures; drop back two and play three measures; drop back two, etc. Variants of this are obvious: play four, drop back two; play four, drop back three; play five, drop back four; etc.
- Practice everything from memory at half tempo.

If you are like most pianists, you will find you can't do many of these tricks. It is precisely at this point that you need to refresh your memory and master the exercise. Doing so will jump-start your confidence, so that the next time you play the music in a normal fashion, it will seem unusually secure and clear in your mind. The theory behind this improvement is that you have clarified the mental signals that trigger your neural and physical responses to a higher level, and the responses feel secure as a result.

Create improvised versions. Amy Faye (1844–1928) was an American pianist who ventured to Europe in the mid-nineteenth century and spent several months in Liszt's master class in Weimar. In her journals, she described one incident of Liszt's playing, stating that "the master" played a wrong note, but he cleverly disguised it by improvising a passage in which the note functioned correctly. Creating improvised versions or easy reductions of the music you play forces you to analyze and organize its basic elements. Once you know them well enough to do this, you establish the feeling that no matter what happens, you can play your way out of it and get back on track. This, in turn, eases your fear of having a lapse, permitting the music to flow so that you will likely never have to use your new-found technique. Music lends itself to this reduction to varying degrees, the more contrapuntal textures being more difficult.

Rehearse memorized performances. This advice seems obvious. Yet those for whom memorizing is challenging tend to cling to the score. Even after music has supposedly been memorized, they leave the score on the music desk because having it there implies security, and its absence generates fear. As each segment or section of the music is memorized, put the music away and practice playing it, linking the sections until the entire piece is memorized. This prevents relegating memorized playing to some later time when the piece is ready to be "tested," creating an event that encourages anxiety. After complete memorization has been achieved, stage trial memorized performances by yourself periodically. These should precede the trial performances for others discussed in the next chapter.

Finally, what if you do have a memory lapse? Human beings are not machines, and it stands to reason that at some point in your professional like, a momentary distraction will result in a memory slip. When it does, do not feed the pattern by dwelling on it or the possibility that it might occur again. Rather, intensify your preparation and discipline your thinking to keep it in perspective, affirming that it was an exception to your usual stability.

Remind yourself that you remember the details necessary to run your life with but an occasional glitch, and you will do so with your music as well. Sometimes maintaining this positive spin takes persistence, especially if your memory lapse took place during a performance that was important to you, or was traumatic for some other reason. Being intrepid in keeping such incidents in perspective and working to ensure they do not happen again is a very important part of your psychological arsenal. If memorization becomes an ongoing part of your regular working pattern, you will over time build a strong technique for it. You will regard it simply as an integral part of your professional life and meet its demands effectively.

11

Handling Rejection . . . and Success

You will not always get what you think you want. Even if you work hard, gear up, and perform well, the results may disappoint you. The teacher you want may turn you down. The school you want may have filled a quota. The prize you want may be awarded to someone else. The grade you want may not be given. And later on, after you get out of school, the job you want may be offered to another candidate. The performance opportunity you want may be granted to another.

Everyone experiences setbacks in seeking both career objectives and life goals. In fact, there is not a person on this planet who has not had to deal with disappointment, probably many times over the years. So you will not be immune from enduring the emotional jolts these moments generate. Given this fact, you need to develop a strategy for dealing with rejection.

First of all, you must protect yourself from thinking that suggests you are not worthy of success. Individuals sometimes believe that somehow the universe holds a grudge against them personally, or that some great force regards them as expendable. This attitude was mentioned in chapter 7. Don't buy into it for even a moment. It may be admirable to be humble and modest, but you must never cross the line and regard yourself as cosmic junk. If you find yourself tempted by this self-deprecation, get tough-minded and exorcise it. Refuse to wallow in this bogus form of humility, for it is only self-pity.

Instead focus on your talent, your hard work, your past successes, and your ability to move others through music. Then mentally embrace your love of music, your emotional response to music, your commitment to sharing music and contributing to a more beautiful world for everyone to live in. Affirm that you were put on this earth as a force to help and to inspire everyone you come in contact with. Believe that you were given this mission, and that carrying it out is your destiny.

Forcing yourself to garner a positive mental attitude after being disappointed is a technique that is very important to practice. As noted before, things are not always going to turn out as you wish, but you can either use these points in your career to get stronger and wiser, or you can let them throw you off course, delaying your recovery to a normal frame of mind and your progress. Moreover, mental patterns feed upon themselves, so if you allow yourself to become depressed and inert as a result of disappointment this time, you will gravitate to the same pattern next time you don't get what you want, probably with greater intensity.

Thus kicking your mind back into a positive mode is your first job. Once you do that, you ought to be objective enough to be able to look at your situation with a healthy attitude. As you do so, focus on some other ideas that will nourish your positive thinking.

First, when you are forced to go another route, remember that you may be better off, for you may not have judged accurately what is best for you. Have faith that the new path will turn out better in the long run, for often rejection saves us from bad choices or leads to better things.

When Johannes Brahms was a rising young pianist, composer, and conductor in his native city of Hamburg, Germany, he applied for the position of conductor of the Hamburg Philharmonic. He was passed over twice, in 1863 and again in 1867. His disappointment led him to accept a conducting post in Vienna, a more powerful cultural center from which he was able to gain more widespread recognition, building his reputation into that of a celebrated musician.

When George Gershwin went to Paris in the 1920s to study composition, he was rejected by both Nadia Boulanger, possibly the most famous Parisian composition teacher of that era, as well as the noted composer Maurice Ravel. Wisely, both declined to teach Gershwin because they felt intense study of classical idioms would adversely affect Gershwin's unique jazz-influenced style. They were right, for the offshoot of these rejections was that Gershwin wrote the orchestra piece *An American in Paris,* which now is an orchestra standard and an audience favorite.

Second, rejection can lead to realizing weaknesses that need attention. As a musician, you cannot escape comparing yourself with others in the profession who strive for the same goals as you. While retaining your basic self-esteem, you can still take stock to learn why you failed. To be sure, sometimes you can never know. Sometimes you represent yourself well and still don't get what you want. In these cases, put it down to experience and move on. Sometimes, the odds are against you. You apply for a position or school and learn that there were many qualified applicants and the spaces are filled.

But sometimes you can figure out what you might have done more effectively. If you really bombed an audition, you understand why you got poor results. Take measures to do better next time. But there might be other factors. Could you have made wiser repertoire choices? If an interview was part of the process, did you think about how to represent yourself? Did you practice speaking about your musical goals, your philosophy as a young artist, or your current professional interests? If you are evaluating your performance in a competition, could you have better prepared yourself for the special circumstances that attend playing in competitions?

Finally, keep your focus on the long haul. The annals of music history report many failures that eventually turned into successes. Musical compositions head the list of first-time flops. Here is a well-known example, the report of a composer who "auditioned" his piano concerto for the famous pianist he hoped would play its first performance:

> I played the first movement. Not a single word, not a single remark! If you knew how stupid and intolerable is the situation of a man who cooks and sets before a friend a meal, which he proceeds to eat in silence! Oh, for one word, for a friendly attack, but for God's sake one word of sympathy, even if not of praise. . . . I fortified myself with patience and played through to the end. Still silence. I stood up and asked, "Well?" Then a torrent poured . . . gentle at first, then more and more growing. . . . It turned out that my concerto was worthless and unplayable; passages were so fragmented, so clumsy, so badly written that they were beyond rescue; the work itself was bad, vulgar; in places I had stolen from other composers; only two or three pages were worth preserving; the rest must be thrown away or completely rewritten. . . . The chief thing I can't reproduce is the *tone* in which all this was uttered. In a word, a disinterested person in the room might have thought I was a maniac, a talented, senseless hack who had come to submit his rubbish to an eminent musician.

The audition was for the famous pianist Nikolai Rubinstein, and the composer was Peter Ilyich Tchaikovsky. The concerto was the composer's first, now arguably the most famous concerto in the world. Tchaikovsky ended this report by angrily vowing never to change a note, although later he did some revision. Get the point?

And this is but one example among many. It is actually amusing to note how wrong critics often were. Here are a few more examples:

- An unknown reviewer wrote in the 1823 publication *The Harmonicon* of Beethoven's piano sonata Op. 111 that "the first (movement) betrays a violent effort to produce something in the shape of novelty" and that "the second movement . . . really is laborious trifling, and ought to be by every means discouraged by the sensible part of the music profession."

- After Robert Schumann's death, his devoted wife, Clara, a celebrated pianist of the day, concertized, playing her husband's music, for she wanted it to become widely known. And indeed, she succeeded, but not without having to face negative reactions in some quarters. She performed *Carnaval* Op. 9 in London in 1856. The review by one H. F. Chorley that appeared in the *Athenaeum* stated, "We can find nothing of the carnival in these fourteen little pieces, which are as insignificant in scale as in a child's lessons, yet without the prettiness and the character which alone make such trifles pass. Uncouth, faded, and wanting in clearness, they seem to us."

- Imagine Chopin's reaction when he read the comments that appeared on November 4, 1843, in London's *Dramatic and Music Review*: "The wildness of both melody and harmony of Chopin is, for the most part, excessive. . . . We cannot imagine any musician, who has not acquired an unhealthy taste for noise, and scrambling, and dissonance, to feel otherwise than dissatisfied with the effect of either of the Third *Ballade*, or the *Grande Valse*, or the Eight *Mazurkas*."

- Arguably, the Rachmaninoff Second Piano Concerto, Op. 18, is the most beloved piano concerto of the twentieth century. Yet when it was played in New York on March 15, 1919, Paul Rosenfeld wrote in the *New Republic*: "Rachmaninoff's Second Piano Concerto is . . . a little too much like a mournful banqueting on jam and honey. . . . In all the music of Rachmaninoff there is something strangely twice-told. From it there flows a sadness distilled by all things that are a little useless. . . . He is still content with music that toys with the pianoforte. . . . There was a day, perhaps, when such work served. But another day has succeeded to it. And so, Rachmaninoff comes amongst us like a very charming and amiable ghost."[1]

---

1. The above quotations and many more are to be found in "Lexicon of Musical Invective" by Nicolas Slonimsky, W. W. Norton, New York, 2000.

These examples illustrate that initial evaluation by those in charge is not always accurate. Sometimes this is because the music is forward-looking and its greatness is not perceived, even by presumably sophisticated listeners. In the case of performances, inaccurate judgments often take place because the window of time is small. Thus the evaluators are not able to perceive enough to make the right choices. Consider, for example, that most auditions and competitions usually last somewhere between ten and twenty minutes. During that time several genres or styles of music are often heard.

You may have the ability to spin a Schubert sonata with great beauty, but your projection of the architecture of such a work is not evident in the short segment of time allotted to your performance. If you feel this is what happened at your last audition, prepare repertoire for the next time that will show your sensitivity in a smaller window of time.

You may be a performer who needs to warm up or settle in before you play your best. If you know this to be the case, then try to offset your penchant for slow warming up by opening your audition with something in your repertoire that is very seasoned, a work with which you can feel comfortable soon after you start to play.

Those in charge might make the wrong decision despite the evidence. History is full of such gaffs. Winning the Prix de Rome was the most important honor a young French composer could receive in the nineteenth century, and, indeed, it was awarded to many composers who later became famous, such as Claude Debussy. But there were also mistakes, if one is to judge by later successes, for both Camille Saint-Saëns and Maurice Ravel were passed over on two separate occasions.

Recognizing that wrong decisions are possible may help you focus on the larger picture. But this reasoning should be tendered with caution. It may alleviate the frustration over not achieving your goal, but it does not excuse you altogether. You still need to examine what might have been better and how you can improve for the next time.

Moreover, unchecked endorsement of assuming the examiners were wrong might keep you from learning something that no one else has been honest or smart enough to identify. It could shock you to think that there may be some truth in negative criticism, especially if it comes in unvarnished commentary. But after the shock subsides, examine what was expressed. Assume the criticism was not motivated by malice. Then ask yourself why, out of all the things that could have been expressed, did the examiner choose to focus on this? What prompted this reaction?

After hearing a young, accomplished pianist play in a master class, a highly revered teacher bluntly noted, "You don't know how to count, do you?" The young pianist bristled at the boldness of the comment. The audience gasped, for the pianist had played his piece with the "correct" rhythm. Had it ended there, the young pianist might have written it off as mistaken judgment, perhaps because the master teacher wanted to justify a reputation for being tough.

What happened next, however, was that the master teacher demonstrated through a series of challenges that the young pianist, indeed, could not count and play the piece at the same time. This inability had resulted in a minimal awareness of how the rhythm of the piece interfaced with the pulse. Thus the performance had been rhythmically correct, but lacked rhythmic vitality. As the pianist overcame his embarrassment and responded to the teacher's exhortations, he began to play the piece with more incisive rhythm and intense excitement. As the new performance unfolded, both he and the audience understood the meaning of the initial comment.

There is yet another reason for avoiding the habit of assuming negative criticism is born of misperception or ulterior motives. Consistently buying into the belief that you are a victim of circumstances can lead to a devastating cynicism you must avoid at all costs. Nothing is more self-defeating than an attitude that assumes those in charge are incompetent at best and corrupt at worst. Even if such assumptions might be valid, harboring them is toxic to your own life view, so, for your own well-being, avoid them. Rather, strike a balance. Realize that mistakes can be made, and perhaps were in your case. But also realize you may be able to do something that will result in a better impression next time.

Dealing with disappointment is difficult for everyone. It is perhaps more so for those who are in the arts, for what you are trying to share with others is very personal, whether it is a performance or a work of visual art. But recognize that others have survived, and many others have used disappointment to become stronger and better. You can too.

Now let us consider a topic that may strike you as strange. Who needs to know how to handle success, how to deal with the good things when they come your way? Obviously, you celebrate and enjoy. Positive feedback strengthens your self-perception, nourishes your creativity, and generates energy for moving ahead. Still, consider these reflections on success.

You may revel in the euphoria you feel over your success, but always be aware of your surroundings when you jump for joy. Sometimes, you can let go without restraint, but at other times you may want to keep your celebration in check, at least until it becomes more private. For example, if you are part of an audience of contestants listening to competition results, you can certainly react with positive pleasure when you learn that you are one of the winners.

Some of those around you will be experiencing disappointment, however, at not having won. They, like you, invested time and effort in their performances, and in many cases what they did was almost as good as your winning performance. Whatever gave you the edge may have been marginal. Thus it behooves you to express your pleasure over your success with enough moderation to keep from seeming to "rub it in."

When you have performed well and are rewarded with accolades, accept the admiration graciously. Do not counter compliments with negativity. This point was discussed in chapter 7, but it bears repeating in this context. If an enthusiastic audience member waxes eloquent over your performance, just go with the flow rather than pointing to some facet of the performance you were not satisfied with. In other words, if someone praises your Mozart, do not apologize for the glitch in the Chopin. Your reluctance to accept praise may well be misunderstood as remoteness or, worse, conceit. Train yourself to regard every comment as significant. When anyone takes the trouble to say something nice, you should take the time to listen and be attentive, with an attitude that returns the goodwill.

Every successful step is important for you, from both a practical and a mental standpoint. Even so, when the rush of having achieved your immediate goal passes, wisdom suggests you regard any single success as part of your long-term plan. Enjoy this positive moment, but remember the journey to becoming the musician, the artist, you want to be is a long one composed of many different phases. Along the way you will celebrate other successes, probably have to deal with disappointments, and most certainly will have to overcome challenges. So celebrate today's victory, but keep it in perspective.

Take a moment to stop and reflect on some of the details that attend today's success. Earmark them in your memory. The conscious awareness of the power you feel in having achieved your goal needs to be stored in a special spot in your being. At some point in the future, remembering it can become useful to you. When you are going through a rough period, you can call it up and draw strength from it; when you need to reassure yourself of your ability to achieve, you can focus on it with the knowledge that you have what it takes to get the job done; and much later, it can trigger a wonderful memory of glorious past times. Reliving your past successes in excess can lead to disillusion with the present, but looking at what you were able to do at some past point can also energize you to achieve even greater success.

12

Choosing Your College

Choosing the right college is an extremely important process. The campus you select is the place you will spend critical years that lead to your goals. Regard this time as precious, a period during which you acquire new information and skills for your profession, learn to interact with others who share your goals, begin to sense how you measure up, and forge your personal career profile.

You undoubtedly dream of specific schools you would like to attend. If you are like most young musicians, however, you will have to temper your thinking by several factors, such as your present level of musical achievement, your academic record, and your financial support. The last is especially important, for ultimately decisions will depend upon what you and your parents can afford. Studying these factors should not lead you to abandon the schools you most want, but rather to consider colleges of varying types and price ranges.

Shopping for a college can be compared with shopping at the mall. You might be able to afford a more expensive item if you find it on sale (i.e., if you get a scholarship). If no sales are available, then you might have to pass up the designer labels (i.e., the prestigious and/or private schools) and look for something of substantial quality at a price you can pay (i.e., schools with a solid reputation that are closer to home or charge lower tuitions, possibly public funded). As with shopping at the mall, you can shop at pricey stores, bargain stores, as well as a few in between.

Aside from these factors, create your college shopping list with your career uppermost in your mind, balancing everything. Seems complicated? Sure, but these different parameters will eventually compress into just a few attractive possibilities. Let's now consider what you need in detail.

INFORMATION AND SKILLS

The most important consideration is finding the right piano teacher for your college years. You already have an idea as to what you want in a teacher (chapter 3), but some new research should take place to find the right teacher for your college years. You may already know the names of the most highly regarded teachers. Your current piano teacher will surely be able to make recommendations. Don't stop there, however. If you enter competitions, examine lists of winners of college-level competitions and note with whom they study. If you hear a performance you like by a young pianist, find out where the person studied and with whom. College and university websites usually contain links to faculty biographies. Look up the names of the faculty piano teachers at the places you are considering and read about them. Then decide which appeal to you most, trying to identify why. If you know of a pianist who studies with a given teacher, try to make contact to ask about experiences with their teacher, tactfully searching for both positive and negative assessments.

As you gather this information, gauge what you are hearing to your own personality, level of achievement, and ability to be challenged. Here are some things to think about:

- How regular is the teacher with regard to lesson meetings? Many teachers have active careers outside the campus, and, indeed, most institutions encourage, even demand, that faculty maintain a high professional profile. Thus some teachers often travel to give concerts, lectures, or master classes. Responsible teachers will see that you get all your lessons, even if there are some scheduling irregularities.

- Does the teacher have a reputation for giving you full attention during your lessons? Teachers who are active professionals sometimes develop the habit of letting personal concerns encroach on lesson time. The result is tardiness, interruptions such as telephone calls, or not focusing effectively on your work at lessons. No matter how elevated the professional reputation of a teacher may be, your lesson time should be used to benefit your musical progress without more than an occasional distraction.

- Does the teacher strike a good balance between challenge and support? Be honest with yourself in reflecting on how you respond to different teaching styles. Some of us get tough and rev up when faced with bluntness. Others get nervous and insecure. Such responses can be changed to some extent with growth and experience, but there is also an underlying personality component within each of us that prompts us to respond to certain types of instructional behavior more than other types. "Tough" teachers are not the best teachers for everyone, nor are "easy" teachers. Most good teachers will strike a balance, and many teachers even change their styles in response to the efforts of the individual student. So consider your own reaction pattern and the teacher's reputation in making a choice.

- Does the teacher have a reputation for inspiring students? Inspiration takes many forms, all of them important. A good teacher

should keep you excited about the music, about working hard
to achieve goals, about planning your career as a professional
musician.

- Does the teacher work with the nuts and bolts of your development: ways to solve technical problems, practice efficiently, memorize securely, and deal with physical or psychological tension?

- How does the teacher regard ancillary musical activities that you
  are pursuing? A good teacher helps you balance your solo work
  with collaboration and other areas that interest you, such as improvisation or composition.

- Does the teacher have a reputation for career counseling? Good
  teachers care about what happens to you professionally. They help
  you envision your niche in the music world and do all they can
  to assist you in achieving your musical and professional goals.
  Your teacher should assess your strengths, counsel you on how to
  maximize them, shore up your weaknesses and advise you when
  making decisions about your career. This counseling should be
  in addition to your lessons for the most part. Beware of teachers
  who have reputations for talking too much at every lesson, rather
  than working with you and your music. A responsible teacher
  finds the time to write recommendations in your behalf at appropriate times and/or make personal contacts with colleagues.

CAMPUS LIFE

Interaction with other students is an important part of college life. For
many, the college experience will be the first time away from home, living
in a community of people their own age. Learning to be an independent,
self-sufficient, successful member of society requires practice, patience,
and sometimes enduring some difficult moments. So, in choosing your
college, consider the campus environment.

There are several types of campuses, so think about where you want
to spend the next years of your life. This choice is not as important as

choosing your piano teacher, and perhaps it will be determined by the previously mentioned financial constraints, but it is still worth consideration. So, what kind of a campus appeals to you? What kind of environment suits your personality and lifestyle?

- The traditional American-style campus is usually clearly defined geographically. Its campus of buildings and open spaces often looks traditional and attractive. Student housing is usually on campus or in the immediate vicinity, and living in a student facility is encouraged. This type of school offers a broad range of degrees, thus attracting students with a variety of professional and academic goals. It also offers an extensive social calendar, boasting fraternities and sororities, hosts major speakers or entertainers, and supports big-time sports events.
- The urban commuter campus may also offer many areas of study but attracts students who commute, many working off-campus for financial support. Student housing may be limited and intertwined with the surrounding city. The campus area is usually much smaller, with structures that resemble office buildings. This campus will offer more limited after-hours events and social opportunities.
- The professional campus is one which, for musicians, is often a conservatory. The range of offerings is highly focused, and interaction is mostly with students who share your interests and goals. The curriculum is narrower, and opportunities to explore a diverse menu of academic topics are fewer, as are chances of meeting others your age who are interested in other fields. Conservatory campuses are traditionally small and tend to be urban, although some are distinctly defined units within a larger university.

Campuses are sometimes a mixture of the three types just described. An important question to consider is how much interaction you want with students who don't share your interests or goals. Pluses and minuses attend this diversity. Some of them are discussed in the next chapter. Also think about the cultural environment surrounding your school. Some people are comfortable with the complexities of urban life, others less so. Advocates point to the opportunities to see, hear, and experience the artistic richness of the city. Others feel such attractions might interfere with the hard work of doing well, believing that campus offerings provide enough cultural opportunities. Some look forward to an active campus social life as an adjunct to studying. Others feel compelled to concentrate mostly on their own development, minimizing social pleasures.

Also research the working environment the university provides for your special needs as a pianist. You might want to read the mission statement of the college or university to determine if there is an underlying political or religious focus and to what extent it impacts student life. Check the availability of practice and rehearsal space and the quality of the pianos you will be practicing on. Check availability of performance space. Some music schools have such a busy recital schedule that being able to find performance space is problematic. So ask about venues when the time comes for you to perform.

Explore what opportunities are offered for you to perform at various points in your study. Inquire if there are master classes by distinguished visitors and the possibility to perform for such artists. Ask about other school-sponsored opportunities to perform. For example, many schools have outreach programs that enable students to present music to schools, assisted living homes, or churches.

These are questions to consider, at least in passing. All of them may not be of equal importance in determining what college to choose, but your personal preferences in these matters might tip the balance in close calls.

GETTING IN

After you decide what colleges to target, you are faced with the flip side: Do they want you? Getting in to one of the colleges on your wish list is often confusing and nerve-racking. The most important preparation is musical, of course. The following is good advice:

- Start planning and preparing for your audition months ahead of time. Check deadlines for applications and prescreening recordings (if required) and plan accordingly.
- Have your repertoire ready weeks before you must play it, either to make a recording or live for a faculty committee. Test it out with trial performances for teachers, family, or friends.
- Read repertoire requirements for the schools you are targeting carefully. If the repertoire you plan does not quite fit the description, contact the school to be sure what you offer will serve to meet the stated requirements. If not, change your plan. Do not assume a repertoire substitution will be overlooked or accepted.
- Most schools require memorization of all audition material. Memorize early, not at the last minute. A good rule is to be giving memorized trial performances at least a month ahead of any recording or performance date. Use the remaining time to polish.
- Choose your repertoire with an eye to seriousness and challenge, but do not try to impress faculty with pieces that are too hard to master or too new to be settled in. Rather, play securely and musically within your present level of achievement.
- In choosing your repertoire, take into account that you will be playing on an unfamiliar instrument, in a strange environment, and that you will probably be nervous.
- Remember that, although faculty members will be assessing your achievement, they will be more interested in what you have to say musically and their perception of your learning potential. If you are able to project intelligence and musicality, you will make a better impression than if you try to dazzle with brilliance and precocity, especially if your attempt to show off is less than solid.

If you spend most of your time in high school becoming the best pianist possible, you might regard your academic work as of secondary importance. Don't be fooled into thinking a great audition will offset a poor high school record. It doesn't and won't at most institutions of higher learning. If you aim to select a school because of its outstanding reputation, you must offer at least a solid academic record, and the more outstanding the better.

Some highly specialized schools, such as music conservatories, sometimes overlook weak academic records if musical talent is strong. Music schools within the framework of a larger institution, on the other hand, must comply with the admissions standards of the university. Thus if your academic record does not meet university requirements, your musical talent will not save the day. To complicate matters, many universities require submission of standardized test scores, such as the SAT for undergraduates or GRE for graduates, as part of the application. Many require minimum score achievement. Moreover, if the university limits its enrollment, then your academic record and test scores will be in competition with those of others who want in, and only the strongest will be accepted.

If you must acknowledge that your high school academic record is poor, prepare yourself for possible rejection. Even so, do not give up. Many students with strong musical talents have been turned down, possibly because in high school they devoted their energy to practicing rather than studying. If you are one of these, look for a community college whose mission is to help students gather enough academic strength to transfer to institutions with more stringent admissions requirements. Many such community colleges have arrangements for their credits to be accepted by larger institutions at the time of transfer. These so-called articulation agreements enable students to prove they can handle college-level academics, while at the same time earning credit that can be transferred. The result is that, although a few credit units may be lost, most credits transfer without significantly delaying graduation.

If you must undergo this detour, you may have to tend to your musical development on the side. Some community colleges have music programs that will support your musical growth, but many do not. Thus often coursework is taken at the community college to prove your academic capability, and at the same time private piano lessons continue with a teacher who can prepare you to transfer at the appropriate musical performance level.

Finally, if your mother tongue is not English, you may have to prove your competence in English through a standard test, such as the TOEFL, or a customized test given by the school you are targeting. Colleges and universities vary in their requirements for this area. Some demand proof of competency for all students whose mother tongue is not English. Others make allowances for prior completion of work in an English-speaking school. Check early to determine both score requirements and to whom they apply.

If you find you must take one or more of these language tests, start preparing early. Most students find them very challenging, even after having resided in the United States and successfully completed school curricula. So do not assume you will be able to breeze through this challenge without special preparation. If you are new to an English-speaking culture, then you should start preparing well in advance of the testing. For most, months of intensive language study will be necessary. Language tests may seem like a minor annoyance for those whose skills are already developed. But in reality many students' plans are delayed significantly by not being able to satisfy the institution of their choice that their English is fluent enough to do university-level work.

TARGETING FINANCIAL HELP

If you want financial support for your college education, you and your family will have to plan with as much diligence as you need to prepare your musical performance. It is naive and ineffective to assume that if you play well enough at your audition, you will be offered the support you need. Institutions never have enough scholarship money, even for the exceptionally talented. So competition for available money is fierce.

Make your financial needs known early to admissions officers. Do not assume you can tap into resources you hear about from others. The scholarship grapevine harbors many half-truths and misconceptions. Moreover, guidelines change constantly, so what may have been true last year or for someone else may not be true this year or apply to you.

You and your parents should schedule a face-to-face conference with an admissions or financial aid official to explore all available options. Aid packages are often complex. Some are based on need, so your family income may be a qualifying factor. Others are based on academic merit, so if your grade average is outstanding, you may qualify for programs that reward such achievement. Others are based on where you reside, with state institutions sometimes offering special support for in-state students. Some target ethnic or cultural groups. With so many variables, you and your parents need to check what can be worked out for your specific situation.

When you confer with the university representative, be prepared and willing to share personal information about family income and existing financial obligations. It is sometimes difficult to be forthright with this information, but it is best to be totally honest to help the financial officer determine what is available. Details that are discussed may have to be documented later, and if the documentation does not support information shared in the conference, then you have wasted both your and the financial adviser's time.

Immigration status is almost always a factor for those students or families who recently arrived in the United States. Proof of additional financial support is often required for foreign students who plan to attend a university in the United States on a visa. Many universities have foreign student specialists who can give you exact information about federal financial expectations. If no such university service exists, then you should contact the federal agency responsible for administering student visa programs.

Although most colleges and universities offer support for academic work, few will offer foreign students the funds they need to obtain visa clearance. Currently that amount is significant, for it presumably covers living expenses for the period of time the visa is valid, and this money must be in escrow before clearance is granted. Working to support yourself after you get here is not a legal option, for in most cases it is prohibited by the terms of the student visa.

With so much to think about and so many unanswered questions, you may become discouraged. But stay the course! Remember, your first job is to get yourself ready. Then set your sights on the schools you want. Many students apply to and audition for as many as four or five universities. Remember to include both those you deem expensive and hard to get into, and those that are more accessible both financially and professionally.

Be vigilant in meeting deadlines. Be patient with yourself, your parents, and the admissions process. Remember that literally thousands enter college and university programs every year despite the trials of the process. Keep the faith! It will happen for you also.

13

Finding Your Way During the College Years

When you start your college education, you will find yourself in a world of those who are at a similar stage of life, embarking on the last segment of education before a professional life. This segment may encompass the better part of a decade if you continue into graduate school, so entering it is a milestone. Also, you are likely to face significant environmental changes. You will experience the following:

- Increased responsibility for your success.
- More choices as to how to use your time and energy.
- More awareness of how you measure up to your peers.
- The need to plan your career and design your education accordingly.

RESPONSIBILITY

You have already taken responsibility for getting your work done in high school. Still, you will be more independent in college, and your responsibility will be more. For example, in high school, many academic classes meet almost every day. In college, classes meet twice or three times a week; a few might meet only once a week. Thus the time you spend in the classroom may be less, perhaps giving the impression that you have a lot of free time every day.

Don't be fooled, for preparation expectations will be much greater, and the burden of meeting such expectations rests on you. You will often be given long-term reading, research, or writing assignments. Their deadlines may seem far in the future, so it is easy to put them off. But preparation often demands many hours, so the burden of starting early and scheduling progress rests on you.

How you budget your time will depend partly on your living arrangement. If you live on or close to campus, you do not spend much time traveling to and from classes. If you commute, you will, of course, have to factor into your schedule the time it takes you to get to and from class. In urban areas, travel time can be considerable.

As a piano student, you should put practice time into your schedule first. You probably know the basics for setting up practicing by now, but it won't hurt to review them as you set up your new schedule.

Practicing every day should hold a high priority. You are now committed to building your education and life around music. So if you have not already established a lifestyle that is focused around working at the piano every day, now is the time to insist on it. Skipping practice on days when you have several classes may be tempting, but remember that, as with physical exercise or dieting, "catching up" on missed days doesn't work well. You may not be able to spend the same amount of time at the piano every day because of your class schedule, but you should try to spend at least some time at the keyboard.

How much is enough? Answer by asking yourself how serious you are about using this precious period of your life to make yourself the best you can possibly be. You may hear about "overpracticing." Yes, it is possible to become so motivated that you practice when you are physically or mentally tired, and, yes, doing so can be counterproductive at best and damaging at worst. But most pianists in college face the opposite challenge: they find it hard to manage three or four hours per day, and they do so only with discipline, fighting for every minute.

Budget your practice time. Know what you want to try to accomplish in each practice session for each piece. Focus your short-term goals on getting ready for your next lesson, and keep in mind long-term goals of piano exams (juries), class performances, or other times you will be performing.

Don't take a practice vacation because your piano professor doesn't get to all the material you are practicing in a given lesson. Many times your teacher will focus on fundamental concepts that will benefit your development as a pianist and musician. So if your lesson is on technique, listening, tone production, phrasing, or pedaling, to name a few possibilities, you are not excused from continuing to prepare the assigned material. Moreover, you now must try to find additional time to perfect the new techniques or ideas you have just learned. This might seem like a lot of pressure initially, but as the new techniques are integrated into your repertoire, new concepts and the music you play begin to coalesce, and the pressure eases.

Even with the best intentions, keeping up with both your coursework and practicing may be extremely difficult. The university system of having a different professor for every course is flawed in that no one professor knows how much work others assign or expect, and often doesn't care. Each professor designs his or her course around learning goals and plans assignments accordingly with no regard for how much work others expect simultaneously. The *only* person who knows the sum of all these assignments is you, and unfortunately, you are not in a position to do much about overload, except to try to manage it.

A well-known academic tradition suggests that most students should spend two to four hours in outside preparation time for each class meeting: two being for easy courses, three for average, and four for hard. Moreover, this expectation is only for routine class meetings. Special reading assignments, papers or reports, quizzes, midterms, or final examinations will demand extra time periodically.

If you are in residence at your university, you may have to plan your scheduling around the availability of practice facilities. At many schools you must sign up for practice rooms, especially if there is high demand for available space. The advantage of such an arrangement is that scheduling your practice time encourages regularity. The downside is that when you face extra academic demands that force you to adjust your schedule, you may not have the flexibility to do so.

WISE CHOICES

Your new life on campus will offer many attractive activities. Although you will be extremely busy meeting your responsibilities, you will need to strike a balance, spending some time in other activities. There will be many choices, some of them compelling. Some are also important to your growth as a human being and your development as a musician. Think about the following:

- Cultivating friends. College friendships often last lifetimes, but building such friendships requires an investment of time. Your immediate friends will probably be from the piano program and music school. Do not, however, overlook the value of making friends from other areas across the campus. General education classes, campus religious groups, clubs, and organizations of various types offer you the opportunity to meet people your own age who have other goals. Getting to know them often opens new perspectives for you, and interacting with them mirrors the diverse community you will live in as an adult. Some friendships have the potential of becoming romances. Learn to be open and pleasant to those you meet on campus, for projecting such a manner is a good life skill to develop.

- Going to concerts. As you are becoming a professional musician, you should go to as many concerts as your schedule will allow. Cultivate the habit of choosing concerts instead of hanging out, watching TV, or socializing online. Concerts give you pleasure and build your knowledge of style and repertoire. This is like making wise food choices. You learn that it is best to choose food that is both good and good for you.

- Taking advantage of cultural opportunities in the area. The benefits of concertgoing should be supplemented by taking time to enjoy museums, theater, art galleries, and lectures that take place either on or off campus. Include events outside your immediate areas of interest, regarding them as adventuresome. You may not like everything you see, hear, or experience, but everything will broaden your understanding of the world in which you live and with which you want to interact as a musician.

- Taking care of yourself. You are young, and if you have normal health for your age, this advice may seem unnecessary. You might find you can stay up all night and still do well the next day, eat whatever junk food you like and feel just fine, never bother to exercise seemingly without consequences. The trouble is that you develop habits that will be hard to change when in later life choosing wise patterns is necessary to stay healthy. Rather, reason that as a performing musician, you depend on your body's physical response. Like an athlete, you should stay in the best possible shape to achieve your personal best. This attitude will pay off, both for now and in the future.

MEASURING UP

Comparing yourself to your peers has been going on to some extent already, but in your college years, you are in close proximity to others who are working for the same goals. Professional achievement and recognition loom in the near future and, for some, will have already begun to take place. As a result, you will be increasingly aware of how your musical efforts compare with those of others. This awareness will likely be in the picture as long as you are professionally active, so forming healthy thinking early in your career as a pianist is important.

Recognize first that the road ahead is long and that life is full of surprises. How you think you compare to others is constantly subject to challenge and change. Each of your peers will make many choices along the way, and these will influence the role each will play. Many times the campus all-stars are not significant members of the profession, and those whose early achievements are more modest emerge among the most admired. So, however you think you compare is constantly changing. Recognize that every individual will pursue a different career path. Learn to focus on tending to yours and let others tend to theirs.

Remind yourself often that you are blessed in being able to work in an art form that is both exciting and beautiful. Be a catalyst for constant celebration of your gift and the gifts of others. Learn to discern quickly what can be praised in the work of others. When you are called upon to offer critical comment, be truthful without being hurtful, and try to supplement your candor with helpful suggestions. Above all, do not become part of a group that harshly criticizes every performance. These cliques of "conservatory mafia" may seem fashionable, but don't get caught up in their constant fault-finding, for such habitual denigration contributes nothing to serious music-making and is often detrimental.

PLANNING A CAREER PROFILE

Although your immediate job will be to learn and grow as much as possible, you should begin to develop a concept of the shape you want your career to take. Performing, both as a soloist and as a collaborator, will certainly be at the heart of what you want to do. Take the time, however, to explore ancillary interests and talents that will add depth to your professional profile. Teaching, lecturing or writing about music, editing, composing, arranging, conducting, creating or managing websites—these are only a few of the possibilities. You probably won't be able to incorporate a lot of them into your life as a performer, but determine which are attractive to you and design your elective curricula with a purposeful focus.

Sometimes, secondary interests develop into significant segments of a musical career. For example, the aforementioned Olga Samaroff, famous for her piano teaching at the Juilliard School of Music, developed a career as a lecturer. Late in her career she instituted a series of music appreciation lectures for the layperson. She became passionate over the importance of educating a broad segment of society to the beauty of classical music. Her lecture series enjoyed several highly successful seasons at Town Hall in Manhattan, and she authored a book based on the series.

The number of music managers, conductors, composer/arrangers, and professionals in all phases of the music industry who were trained as pianists is legion. This fact should not invalidate or even mitigate the ambition you feel during your college years for becoming the best pianist possible, for this challenge represents your first love and should be the most important job at this stage of your career. Still, beginning to plan at this time how you can broaden what you have to offer the profession is something that you should undertake. Chapter 16 will elaborate on this topic in some detail.

Consciously enjoy the time you spend on a college campus. There may never be another time in your life when you are as free to concentrate on the things that are the most important to you personally. This is the time for you to find your way as a musician and as an adult. Be good to yourself by building both your art and your lifestyle carefully.

14

Planning Repertoire

You will expand your knowledge of piano literature for as long as you are a pianist. This repertoire is both vast and fascinating. Fortunately, many of the geniuses of Western music were keyboard players and created some of their most beautiful music for their own instrument. A partial list of such giants includes Scarlatti, all the Bach family, Mozart, Beethoven, Schubert, Mendelssohn, Chopin, Schumann, Liszt, Brahms, Debussy, Ravel, Rachmaninoff, Scriabin, Prokofiev, Albéniz, Granados, and Bartók. Although earlier composers wrote for predecessors of the piano or early versions of today's instrument, their keyboard music is played in piano recitals so often that most professionals and audiences accept playing harpsichord and fortepiano music on modern-day instruments. Along with music of the more famous composers is a large repertoire by composers whose place in music history is less exalted, but who wrote piano music that is worth exploring and playing. This repertoire offers opportunities to create programs of music that is not heard often but is colorful and exciting.

Although you accumulate knowledge of this repertoire your entire career, the years during which you receive your professional education are perhaps the most exciting for discovering new literature. You become acquainted with new sounds and personalities, and newly discovered music seems fresh and wonderful. Some music is by composers whose styles you already know. You may have played a few preludes and fugues by Bach, but you can discover the rest of these forty-eight masterpieces, as well as many other large bodies of the literature, such as the sonatas of Haydn and Mozart, or the thirty-two piano sonatas of Beethoven, not to mention dozens of works by the major nineteenth- and twentieth-century composers. You will not play all this material, but you will get to know it as a listener, amassing a mental library of music from which to build your programs.

A good teacher will encourage you to explore this treasure trove of repertoire and help you choose music that is both challenging and gratifying to learn. You should, however, explore on your own as much as possible. Keep a notebook of pieces that are attractive as you hear them in recitals or on CDs. Spend some computer time exploring and downloading music by composers whose names are new to you. Did you hear someone mention names like Szymanowski, Medtner, or Mompou? Find some performances online to see if you like their music. Did you hear one of your friends talk about minimalist music? What does that mean? Listen to some piano works by minimalist composers. In becoming acquainted with new kinds and styles of music, you don't have to like everything the moment you hear it. But you do need to expand your musical horizons, and doing so will broaden your musical tastes as well.

Find out who is creating new music around you. Young composers are always grateful for performers who learn and play their music. Become such a performer as much as time allows. You might suspect that doing so means learning music that is not on the same level as that of recognized masterpieces. This might be true, but such will be offset by the energy you will feel from the creativity of your generation. And you never know what will happen to the music you premiere. One suspects that pianist Ricardo

Viñes (1875–1943) did not know his first performances of piano pieces by Debussy and Ravel would become a part of music history.

Moreover, working with composers can teach you much about their creative processes. Although not all composers think the same way, you will still be able to identify creative patterns that you can relate to the work of composers from the past. Your suggestions as a performer can even inspire composers to revise their music in various ways, giving you even more special insights.

As you begin building your repertoire, you may feel a special affinity with certain composers or periods of music. Not only do you love this music, but you find its stylistic subtleties mesh with your own temperament. You may also find that other repertoire or styles will be harder to bring to the same level of excellence. As you develop an understanding of your own strengths and challenges, you should both emphasize the styles you are naturally good at and buckle down to strengthen those that seem more remote.

You find, for example, that you are totally comfortable with the music of Johann Sebastian Bach. You learn it easily and feel secure playing it. You garner praise from both your teacher and peers for your performances. They admire you for being a "Bach player." You are also aware that some of your friends have a more difficult time playing Bach, and a few of them fear the challenges inherent in contrapuntal textures. Thus you decide to learn as much as possible of the *Well-Tempered Clavier* and become a Bach specialist. This is good, intelligent planning.

By the same token, you know that your Debussy is weak. You haven't played much of his music, but when you do, your teacher talks to you in terms you do not easily understand, such as "color," or "balancing sonority," "nonarticulated textures," "half damping," and "half pedaling." You also find this music more difficult to memorize. You know two of your classmates who soak up this style and whose playing of it inspires comments like "atmospheric" or "beautifully tinted." You decide you aren't comfortable with French impressionism and avoid learning this music. This is poor planning that will ultimately compromise your flexibility as a professional musician.

The best strategy, of course, is to combine the two approaches. Become a Bach specialist, by all means, but also develop enough affinity for Debussy to include representative examples in your repertoire, teach it effectively, and adjudicate others' performances of it. This example could be applied to any two periods of music or styles. Most composers' styles will fall somewhere in between these two hypothetical extremes. As a professional musician, you should understand as many different styles as possible to work effectively with whatever music crosses your path. In achieving this goal, work constantly for balance, perfecting what you do well and strengthening areas that are difficult. Each process has its rewards: exhilaration living in the rarefied world of the specialist, and pride in overcoming tough challenges.

As you build repertoire, you will devote most of your attention to learning and perfecting new pieces. You may have to play new material for faculty regularly during your college years. Your grades partially depend on the success of these "juries." Thus, as juries approach, your focus will be on the material you have just learned, for you want to play it well. There are, however, times when performance deadlines are not imminent. Use these times to explore new repertoire and start new works, activities most musicians find fun and exciting.

Also use part of this "down" time to refresh works that you have played earlier. Decide what works you want in your permanent repertoire and review them often enough to keep them in your fingers and head. Indeed, you should know a few pieces, perhaps half a dozen, well enough to be able to play them anytime, anywhere. Works become this secure after they have been reviewed several times over a period of months. Having them ready to go is an obvious advantage when you are unexpectedly called upon to play. Occasionally such circumstances end up being important for your career, so you should always be ready. And even in ordinary situations, you cannot afford to be a pianist who has nothing ready to play.

There are three other balancing acts you should incorporate into your repertoire planning. The first concerns the difficulty of the repertoire you choose. At one end of the spectrum is the repertoire that presents significant challenges. This repertoire is exciting partly because it is reputed to be hard. Indeed, you may believe that if you perform this music well, the effect will be stunning. At the other end of the spectrum is repertoire that is easily within range, attractive but unlikely to wow everyone simply by your having managed to play it.

You should include both types. Obviously, if you never challenge yourself, you never experience the growth and excitement that result from such daring. But these works tend to require continuing intense practice. If you load yourself with too many, you run the risk of not devoting enough attention to any one of them to achieve the performance standard you want. Thus, as you build programs and permanent repertoire, pace your challenges. Stretch sometimes, but also include more comfortable works.

The second balancing act has to do with musical content. At one end of the spectrum are serious, monumental works: sonatas, long sets of variations, multisectional toccatas or fantasias, or piano tone poems. At the other end are short, light pieces, often charming, but without serious intent. Include both types in your repertoire. A recital program usually contains at least one or two longer, more serious works, so you will need to have these as staples. Sometimes the second type is also included in a recital, usually after intermission. Whether or not the lighter pieces become part of your recital program, they should be in your repertoire. On occasion, you will play for an audience that is not prepared to listen to a twenty-minute sonata or a fifteen-minute set of variations. At these times, be ready to play music that offers a few minutes of easy-listening pleasure.

The third balance is one that concerns those who plan to enter competitions. Some repertoire has a reputation for being effective in competitions. This reputation may be substantiated by observing the repertoire past winners have played. Examples in solo repertoire are the more popular sonatas of Beethoven, such as the Opp. 53 and 57, or virtuoso works of the nineteenth century, by composers such as Liszt and Chopin. The twentieth century also has its champions, such as examples drawn from works of Rachmaninoff, Prokofiev, Bartók, Barber, or Ravel. In the concerto category, winners have often prepared brilliant works by composers such as Chopin, Liszt, Brahms, Tchaikovsky, Prokofiev, or Rachmaninoff. If you plan to enter competitions, you may lean toward selecting pieces you believe will help you win. Even so, balance your overall repertoire by learning more introspective works that contribute to your long-term growth as a musician, even if you choose not to use them in competitions.

Moreover, increasingly competition veterans realize that adjudicators are often impressed by the daring of choosing works that do not have obvious audience appeal. Thus introspective works are appearing in competition programs with increasing frequency.

Do not neglect learning concerted music. During your college years, you should plan to study at least one piano concerto every year, so when you graduate you will have several in your repertoire. As noted in chapter 6, working with this repertoire develops listening and ensemble skills that might otherwise remain dormant. Moreover, since opportunities to play with an orchestra are likely to be infrequent, you need to be able to offer several concertos from your repertoire if you are lucky enough to be offered such a performance.

In addition, you should always be participating in at least one substantial collaboration. The chamber and vocal repertoire with piano contains some of the most glorious music ever written. Learning and playing this repertoire is one of the most joyful, valuable experiences a pianist can have. As noted in chapter 6, your collaborators will often be able to offer insights into the music that will strengthen everything you do as a pianist. Singers and other instrumentalists often view music with a somewhat different perspective, and working with them opens new ways of thinking. Discussions among collaborators can sometimes be lively and intense, but if those involved are dedicated to creating the best possible performance, everyone benefits. Once in a while you may encounter collaborators who are not creative and flexible. If you do, just trade them in for musicians who are more amiable.

Planning and building repertoire is one of the most enjoyable aspects of musical life. In this chapter we have focused on how to build and balance repertoire. In the next, let's go to the repertoire supermarket to get some idea of what you can shop for.

15

Selecting Repertoire

Now that you have some ideas about how to build and balance your repertoire, let's look at what's out there. Our trip through the repertoire supermarket will observe chronology (what was written when) and centrality (what is important in your development as a professional musician), probable effectiveness with your audience, and some advice about editions to look for. When you shop at the supermarket, you only buy what you can use in the immediate future, even if you see lots of items you may want to try later, but if you plan ahead, you can eventually partake of a multitude of items. It is the same with repertoire. Start with only a few things; combine what is attractive with what you need. Build and balance over the years.

SOLO REPERTOIRE SUMMARY

Category: Seventeenth- and Eighteenth-Century French Harpsichord Music

Centrality: Very important for harpsichordists, not as much for pianists.

Representative composers: François Couperin (1668–1733);
Jean-Philippe Rameau (1683–1764).

What: Short pieces in collections or suites, some with descriptive
titles like "The Flies," "The Little Windmills," "The Chatter of
Birds," "The Floating Bonnet," etc. A few longer pieces, often
variations.

Effect: Interesting and charming; nice vignettes, used often as
encores.

Editions: Nineteenth-century editors usually incorporate piano
techniques such as the use of damper pedal or piano touch
forms. Later editions are closer to sources, but most pianists
will need editorial help realizing ornamentation.

What to learn: If you find these appealing, six or more pieces, or
a set of variations.

Category: Late Seventeenth-Century and Early Eighteenth-Century Spanish Harpsichord Music

Centrality: Pianists have adopted this repertoire, for it is challenging and effective.

Representative composers: Domenico Scarlatti (1685–1757); Antonio Soler (1729–1783).

What: About 550 one-movement "sonatas" of Scarlatti; 150 one
or more movement sonatas of Soler.

Effect: Sparkling and vital, often with technical display: skips,
repeated notes, and rapid passage work.

Editions: The complete Scarlatti sonatas edited by Alessandro
Longo (1864–1945) are burdened with editorial additions.
Ralph Kirkpatrick (1911–1984) completed a critical edition
of Scarlatti's complete works in 1953, offering unadorned
scores of about sixty of the sonatas and revising Longo's
order, setting a standard most later editors follow in sub-
sequent collections. Soler's sonatas are available in various
collections, notably those edited critically by Frederick
Marvin.

What to learn: Two or three sonatas a must, more if you find
   them fun. Great audience appeal.

Category: High Baroque Keyboard Music of the Late Seventeenth and Eighteenth Centuries

Centrality: Fundamental for the pianist's development and reper-
   toire despite being written for earlier instruments.
Representative composers: Johann Sebastian Bach (1685–1750):
   George Frideric Handel (1685–1759).
What: Teaching pieces, dance suites, preludes and fugues, toccatas, various other works.
Effect: Both composers represent the epitome of the Baroque and
   are considered among the greatest geniuses of Western music.
Editions: Avoid editions with many additions (some by famous
   musicians, such as Czerny, Mugellini, Busoni). Many recent
   critical editions are available. Hans Bischoff created an early,
   still serviceable critical edition, which is inexpensive in reprints.
What to learn: Bach is more significant as a keyboard composer
   than Handel. To develop your pianistic skills, work on Bach's
   teaching pieces, including several two- and three-part inventions.
   Sample other types: two or three suites drawn from the French
   and English sets or the partitas; learn at least half a dozen preludes and fugues from the *Well-Tempered Clavier* (sample both
   volumes); at least one toccata; one other work such as the "Italian" concerto, Chromatic Fantasy and Fugue, or the Capriccio on
   a Departed Brother. If you adore Bach, undertake the Goldberg
   Variations. At some point you should explore a Handel suite.

Category: Classical Piano Music of the Eighteenth and Early Nineteenth Centuries

Centrality: Some of the greatest and most performed works in
   Western classical music; necessary for your musical development and repertoire.

Representative composers: Carl Philipp Emanuel Bach (1714–
    1788); Franz Joseph Haydn (1732–1809); Wolfgang Amadeus
    Mozart (1756–1791); Ludwig van Beethoven (1770–1827).
What: Sonatas, sets of variations, fantasias, miscellaneous pieces;
    especially important are the fifty-two sonatas of Haydn; nine-
    teen of Mozart; thirty-two of Beethoven (plus three early ones).
Effect: This is all great music, ranging from charming small to
    monumental works, from lighthearted to profound. Perform-
    ers and audiences revel particularly in favorites of Mozart and
    Beethoven, but C. P. E. Bach and Haydn are programmed with
    increasing frequency.
What to learn: Works by all composers. Don't overlook the har-
    monic boldness of late C. P. E. Bach or regard Haydn as easier
    or less important, for especially the last thirty sonatas are a
    treasure trove of wonderful, expressive music. Plan to learn
    at least one piece by C. P. E. Bach and two Haydn sonatas, or
    try the F minor variations. Mozart offers his own incompa-
    rable rewards. Plan to include at least three sonatas in your
    repertoire, as well as at least one set of variations. Beethoven
    moves from high classicism into early romanticism. His sona-
    tas are so essential to your development as a pianist that you
    will continue to study and play them your entire career, cer-
    tainly learning five or six, possibly double that number. Many
    pianists make a project out of learning and performing all
    thirty-two of them. His variations range from light, entertain-
    ing works to monumental works such as the Op. 35 ("Eroica")
    and Op. 120 ("Diabelli") sets. A popular attractive set is the 32
    Variations (WoO 80).

Category: Piano Music of Less Frequently Heard Composers of the Turn of the Nineteenth Century

Centrality: This music offers worthwhile alternatives to more fre-
    quently heard repertoire. Although still not in the mainstream,

it is currently being reexamined and revived. Your involvement should reflect personal interest and attraction.

Representative composers: Muzio Clementi (1752–1832); John Field (1782–1837); Carl Maria von Weber (1786–1826); Johann Nepomuk Hummel (1778–1837); Carl Czerny (1791–1857).

What: Clementi, 100+ sonatas and sonatinas; Field, sixteen nocturnes; Weber, four sonatas and show pieces; Hummel, sonatas and fantasias; Czerny, sonatas, variations, and a famous early motor toccata.

Effect: Varied because of lack of familiarity and uneven interest; best examples convey the excitement of discovery and early Romantic virtuosity or sentiment.

Editions: Shop for recent critical editions rather than nineteenth-century reprints.

What to learn: Representative examples of music that interests and excites you.

Category: Nineteenth-Century Piano Music of the Romantic Period

Centrality: The period in which the piano becomes of age, and the literature written for it remains at the heart of the repertoire, combining emotional intensity with virtuosity.

Representative composers: Franz Schubert (1797–1828); Felix Mendelssohn (1809–1847); Frederick Chopin (1810–1849); Robert Schumann (1810–1856); Franz Liszt (1811–1886); Johannes Brahms (1833–1897).

What: Poetic virtuosic pieces with titles such as Ballade, Barcarolle, Berceuse, Capriccio, Etude, Fantasia, Impromptu, Intermezzo, Novelette, Prelude, Rhapsody, or Scherzo. Many, especially of Schumann and Liszt, carry descriptive titles derived from art or literature, and some are combined to form longer works or sets of pieces. Older forms such as the sonata or sets of variations are still extant, especially in the works of

Schubert and Brahms, but the number of works in these traditional forms is much smaller. Some of the older forms experience metamorphosis, such as the sonata in the hands of Liszt.
Because virtuosity is emphasized in this period, the etude designed to develop technique becomes important as a concert
piece. Also frequently encountered are paraphrases on music
borrowed from opera or other sources, combining music familiar to audiences of the day with virtuoso display.

Effect: Audiences and performers revel in this literature, and it
remains the most frequently performed.

Editions: Much of this music was published and edited in the
nineteenth century. These editions still serve many performers. Critical editions appearing in the twentieth century are
usually more reliable, for they are typically free from editorial
additions.

What to learn: You will be learning as much of this music as possible for your entire career as a pianist.

Category: French Piano Music of the Late Nineteenth and Twentieth Centuries

Centrality: A staple in the repertoire of all pianists, and a primary focus for those attracted to it.

Representative composers: Gabriel Fauré (1845–1924); Claude
Debussy (1862–1918); Maurice Ravel (1875–1937); Francis
Poulenc (1899–1963); Olivier Messiaen (1908–1992).

What: Individual pieces, presented sometimes in sets. They
often carry descriptive titles that reference nature, antiquity,
or poetry. They vary in length and difficulty but are noted for
exploiting the sonority of the piano by using complex harmonies and pedal effects. Fauré and Poulenc use traditional genre
titles often (impromptu, barcarolle, etc.), the others more
sporadically.

Effect: Music awash in sonority, with "color" that arises from
using the damper pedal to create complex harmonic combinations. Slow, soft music can range from being sentimental
(Debussy's *Clair de lune*) to stark (Ravel's *Le Gibet*). Rhythmic
patterns are often borrowed from other cultures, frequently
from Spain. Some pieces present significant virtuosic demands, particularly those of Ravel and Messiaen.

Editions: Original publications are available for most of this
music, most of it without pedal indications. Later editors
frequently add these, as well as ways to address technical
problems.

What to learn: You certainly should have six or seven pieces of
Debussy and Ravel in your repertoire. If you resonate with
this special music, the sky is the limit.

Category: Russian Piano Music of the Nineteenth and Twentieth Centuries

Centrality: Russia developed a strong musical voice in the late
nineteenth and twentieth centuries. Many of her most gifted
composers were pianists. Thus a vast, challenging, and colorful literature has become a distinct, powerful staple for pianists everywhere.

Representative composers: Modest Mussorgsky (1839–1881);
Pyotr Ilyich Tchaikovsky (1840–1893); Alexander Scriabin
(1872–1915); Sergei Rachmaninoff (1873–1943); Nikolai
Medtner (1880–1951); Serge Prokofiev (1891–1953); Dmitri
Kabalevsky (1904–1987); Dmitri Shostakovich (1906–1975).

What: Traditional genre types predominate: etudes, preludes, sonatas, fugues, variations, fantasias, poems. Shorter pieces with
nonmusical references also appear, particularly associated
with Mussorgsky ("Pictures at an Exhibition"), Tchaikovsky
("The Seasons"), and the teaching pieces of Kabalevsky.

Effect: This body of literature has great audience appeal because it is typically virtuosic, full of colorful sonorities, and intensely emotional. It is an extension of the European Romantic tradition, although much of it was written in the twentieth century. Its popularity with both pianists and audiences has resulted in much of it being well known, except for the works of Medtner, which are rapidly being discovered, and some late works of Scriabin.

Editions: Most of this music is available in original editions. Some later publications incorporate editorial markings or suggestions.

What to learn: Like the nineteenth-century Romantic literature, this body of music is essential to every pianist's repertoire. Learn as much as you can.

Category: Spanish and South American Piano Music of the Late Nineteenth and Twentieth Centuries

Centrality: The popularity of this music is on the rise, and most pianists include representative examples of it in their repertoire. A few specialize in it.

Representative composers: Isaac Albéniz (1860–1909); Enrique Granados (1867–1916); Manuel de Falla (1876–1946); Joachín Turina (1882–1949); Heitor Villa-Lobos (1887–1959); Federico Mompou (1893–1987); Alberto Ginastera (1916–1983).

What: Descriptive pieces of varying length based on nationalistic rhythmic and melodic characteristics, often in virtuosic settings. Mompou is famous for miniatures; Turina and Ginastera sometimes used traditional genres, such as the sonata. Some pieces of Turina, Villa-Lobos, and Ginastera are often used for teaching.

Effect: This music is attractive to both performers and audiences; it is usually colorful, easy listening, pianistic; some of it is technically difficult.

Editions: Most of this music is available in original editions. Some of it has been edited, especially those works used in the teaching studio.

What to learn: Include at least three or four representative examples in your repertoire, and if this music attracts you, add more over time.

Category: Other European Composers of the Late Nineteenth and Twentieth Centuries

Centrality: Varies with composer, some being very important for your development and repertoire, others less so. The most important are highlighted with boldface here.

Representative composers: **César Franck** (1822–1890); Biedrich Smetana (1824–1884); Antonin Dvořák (1841–1904); **Edvard Grieg** (1843–1907); Leoš Janáček (1854–1928); Max Reger (1873–1916); **Béla Bartók** (1881–1945); **Karol Szymanowski** (1882–1937); **Paul Hindemith** (1895–1963).

What: Types vary depending on the composer. Franck is known for but one important work, Prelude Chorale and Fugue; Grieg and Bartók for smaller nationalistic pieces, sometimes in sets; there are one or more sonatas of Grieg, Bartók, Szymanowski, and Hindemith. Of the less performed composers, Smetana, Janácek, and to some extent Dvořák represent middle-European nationalism; Reger wrote two monumental sets of variations and smaller Brahms-like pieces.

Effect: Grieg and Bartók are favorites with audiences; the others are easily accessible to listeners and should be well received, exceptions being later Szymanowski and all of Hindemith, both of whom write in a less emotionally intense style with moderate dissonance.

Editions: Earlier works are apt to be updated by editors. Later ones are usually available in original editions.

What to learn: Representative pieces by highlighted composers are standard repertoire fare. Other composers represent
byways from mainstream literature, but exploring them allows
you to perform music that is unfamiliar and often exciting. Be
adventuresome and choose a few.

Category: Nontonal or Dissonant Piano Music of the Early
and Mid-Twentieth Century

Centrality: Although this music is historically important, most
pianists don't play much of it. A few become specialists in it.
Representative composers: Arnold Schönberg (1874–1951);
Anton Webern (1883–1945); Alban Berg (1885–1935); Pierre
Boulez (b. 1925); Karlheinz Stockhausen (1928–2007)
What: Earlier composers wrote relatively little for piano: Schön-
berg about twenty small pieces; Webern a short work called
Variations; Berg a one-movement sonata; Stockhausen about a
dozen pieces of varying length; Boulez three sonatas and a few
pieces.
Effect: Audiences often don't understand this music and respond
coolly to it, despite the fact that it is extremely difficult to play.
Memorization is so challenging that it is often performed with
the score.
Editions: Original editions are available and used for performance preparation.
What to learn: Explore whatever attracts and challenges you.

Category: Piano Music by United States Composers
of the Late Nineteenth Century and Twentieth Century

Centrality: Varies from well-known, popular works that are important in the repertoire to infrequently played works.

Representative composers: Edward MacDowell (1860–1908);
Charles Ives (1874–1954); Charles Tomlinson Griffes (1884–
1920); Aaron Copland (1900–1990); Samuel Barber (1910–
1981); Norman Dello Joio (1913–2008); Vincent Persichetti
(1915–1987).

What: A vast array of piano music of all types; each of the composers wrote one or more sonatas

Effect: Attractive and often exciting, ranging from the late Romantic style of MacDowell through the moderately dissonant
style of later composers.

Editions: Original editions are usually available.

What to learn: You should have representative pieces in your
repertoire, and some works, such as the Barber sonata or the
Copland variations, are very popular and effective.

The foregoing is a cursory overview of what is available to learn and perform. This survey contains more than enough for one lifetime of listening
and study. Even so, you should continue to explore as both old and new
piano music surfaces. Research and technology serve to make available
literally thousands of scores. It is exhilarating and rewarding to play "un-
discovered" piano works. Here is a representative list of composers from
past eras whose music is worth digging out:

Manuel Blasco de Nebra (1750–1784): Short Scarlatti-like keyboard sonatas.

Johann Jakob Froberger (1616–1667): His Baroque dance suites
influenced those of J. S. Bach.

Johann Christian Bach (1735–1782): A gifted son of J. S. Bach
who wrote in an early classical style.

Jan Ladislav Dussek (1760–1812): Classical sonatas, fantasias.

Ignaz Moscheles (1794–1870): Knew Beethoven and Chopin; his
concert etudes are attractive.

Fanny Mendelssohn Hensel (1805–1847): Romantic pieces;
many found her as gifted as her brother Felix.

Ferdinand Hiller (1811–1885): Sonatas and early Romantic
pieces.

Charles-Valentin Alkan (1813–1888): Famous virtuoso pianist
who wrote show pieces.

Stephen Heller (1813–1888): Highly regarded by contempo-
raries, Schumann-like short pieces;

Adolf von Henselt (1814–1889): His early etudes deemed harder
than those of Chopin

Clara Wieck Schumann (1819–1896): Her short pieces compare
favorably with those of her husband, Robert.

Joachim Raff (1822–1882): Highly regarded in the nineteenth
century; two piano sonatas and shorter pieces.

Anton Rubinstein (1829–1894): One of the greatest pianists of
his time; short Romantic pieces.

Camille Saint-Saëns (1835–1921): Etudes and other short pieces;
his five concertos still performed often.

Jules Massenet (1842–1912): Although known as an opera composer, he wrote many piano pieces.

Moritz Moszkowski (1854–1925): Cleverly written etudes and
show pieces.

Cécile Chaminade (1857–1944): One sonata, etudes, many character pieces.

Sergei Lyapunov (1859–1924): 12 Transcendental Etudes to complete the cycle of keys started by Liszt.

Anton Arensky (1861–1906): Sets of etudes and preludes.

Ferruccio Busoni (1866–1924): Twenty-four preludes; other
pieces harmonically complex and contrapuntal.

Ernst von Dohnányi (1877–1960): Sets of character pieces;
rhapsodies.

Be especially vigilant to explore recently created music. There is so much
fascinating music in this category that an overview is impossible. A few
suggestions of composers' works to explore are those of William Bolcom
(etudes and rags); John Cage (prepared piano pieces); Elliott Carter (sonata

and other pieces); Henry Cowell (pieces using clusters and inside the piano); George Crumb (suites using both keyboard and inside the piano); John Corigliano (Fantasy etudes and pieces); Henri Dutilleux (sonata and pieces); Ross Lee Finney (sonatas and pieces); Lowell Liebermann (*Gargoyles* and other pieces); György Ligeti (etudes); Frank Martin (preludes); Donald Martino (preludes and *Pianississimo*); Robert Muczynski (sonatas and suites); Toru Takemitsu (coloristic pieces); Carl Vine (sonatas).

Never stop expanding your knowledge of the glorious literature that has been written for the piano. Such a treasure trove provides one of the greatest joys attending your art.

16

Broadening Horizons

Olga Samaroff has been mentioned several times in earlier chapters as a pianist who taught at the Juilliard School of Music in New York City in the mid-twentieth century. She enjoyed a worldwide reputation, having taught several high-profile pianists of that era, notably William Kapell, Rosalyn Tureck, and Eugene List. Since New York City was a center for concert management, she was acutely aware of how hard it is for young musicians to find a niche in the professional world. She often counseled them, stating that obviously the first great challenge was to master performing, to become an artist. Then she pointed to a second challenge, more formidable than the first: that after years of spending effort, money, and time to becoming an artist . . . *no one cared.*

Overcoming the second challenge is even harder today than it was decades ago when Samaroff made her observation. Part of the reason for this is that in recent years technology has placed at our fingertips a multitude of attractive diversions. Traditional forms of entertainment such as attending concerts are upstaged by the immediacy and excitement of computer games, social networks, and other ephemeral activities. Listening to music of any kind, but especially listening to classical music, demands abstract conceptualization and a sustained attention span, skills that have been eroded by the immediacy and kaleidoscopic capabilities of technology. Thus audiences for classical music have become small, consisting mostly of those who love to study and perform it, their families, and friends.

If you are not financially independent from sources outside your musical pursuits, you must recognize the difficulty inherent in earning your living with music without becoming discouraged. But you must also plan to deal with this challenge. To do so, you should prepare to be as versatile as possible, using your strengths and interests to offer a variety of services that supplement your role as a performing pianist. The earlier you can forge an individual profile and begin ancillary training, the better you will be when the time comes to end your education and make the transition to the workaday world.

You may feel that focusing on anything but becoming the best pianist you can robs your development and weakens your main purpose. To some extent this concern is valid, for there are only so many hours in the day and by now you realize that you have a monumental task bringing your pianism up to an artistic level. Still, you cannot afford to stand before the world, diploma(s) in hand, wondering what will happen next. For, as noted at the beginning of this chapter, likely *nothing* will happen, and the resulting feeling of dismay has the power to defeat you altogether.

Thus, as with so many issues, you must create a balance, finding room for . . . well, what? Your first task is to discover what interests and talents you have that can be developed to give you the breadth you need, as well as some degree of personal satisfaction. As you scan your psyche, note the following possibilities. Most famous musicians love to teach the next generation. A few examples are J. S. Bach, Haydn, Mozart, Beethoven, Chopin, Liszt, Bartók, Hindemith, Schoenberg, and Stravinsky. Some were church musicians: J. S. Bach (again), Franck, Fauré, Messiaen, Some devoted substantial amounts of time to posts that required administrative skills: J. S. Bach (still), Mendelssohn, Liszt, Fauré. Others earned part of their living as conductors: Mendelssohn, Brahms, and Rachmaninoff. Still others were expert collaborators: Brahms, Debussy, Ravel. A few loved music journalism: Schumann, Berlioz, Debussy. The point is that *most* musicians of the past sustained careers that combined several activities. This was partly to earn a living, to be sure, but also many discovered the diversity itself nourished the art they loved and practiced.

The list of possible combinations is almost endless. Here are a few to look into, not at a later time, but rather *now* while you continue to pursue your pianistic goals. You won't want to try to become expert in all of these ancillary skills. Rather, take time to explore and develop those that interest you, staying open-minded to the possibility that an area you don't know anything about may become even more attractive as your knowledge of it grows.

- Hone your skills as a teacher. Take pedagogy courses. Get acquainted with learning theories. Examine and evaluate contemporary teaching methods and materials. Observe various teaching situations: master classes, group piano sessions for beginners, school music classes for children. Your goal is to develop expert teaching skill supplemented with a knowledge of learning theories and teaching materials at all levels. You thus become a prime candidate for being hired to teach at a music school, whatever level its clientele. Take elective courses in business, so you learn how to run and market a piano studio.

Success story: A young woman found the time during her college career as a pianist to incorporate training in business practices and marketing. After she graduated, she started a piano studio in an affluent suburb of a major city, putting her business skills into practice. In five years her piano studio grew to a profitable music school for which she gradually hired a dozen other teachers

- Become a voice for music through the written word. Start by practicing writing until you know how to write fluently and effectively. Just a few years ago, you had to try to spread your word through a published journal, be it a news column, music criticism, or scholarly research. Blogging now makes it possible to set forth your ideas immediately to potentially a vast audience. Blogging doesn't necessarily pay, of course, but it can lead to a broad reputation if you write consistently and interestingly. Employment opportunities often follow such recognition.

Success story: A young pianist recently graduated from a conservatory in her native China. She immigrated to the United States and found that little was known about piano music written by contemporary Chinese composers. She wrote a weekly blog that highlighted such music, and, after receiving appropriate permission, put up musical excerpts. Her following spread from Chinese pianists, to the larger Chinese community, and finally to the piano community at large. The reputation she built through the blog nourished a successful, multifaceted career as a collaborator, independent teacher, and competition administrator.

- Put your creativity to work to seek out markets that need what you have to offer and overcome whatever reticence you might have to ask for funding from philanthropic organizations. In this context, learn how to ferret out such organizations and deal with (often formidable) grant applications. Become experienced in grant writing. Even if you harvest but modest results, you can make substantial contributions to the cultural life of your community, and your services will be sought by many organizations. Take note that many philanthropic organizations look favorably on proposals that foster the education of children and young adults.

Success story: A young pianist learned that the public schools in his community had discontinued music programs because of budget cuts. To address this vacuum, he conceived an after-school music program and underwent the arduous process of applying for support from several regional foundations. He received funding to start his program in a number of schools, moving throughout the school district with portable keyboards. The program was applauded by both parents and school officials. He expanded support for the program by giving piano recitals to raise supplemental funds. Recently he was honored for outstanding community service at a public event, and he has become an icon for music study in the minds of many.

- Build a collaborative repertoire in an area that you enjoy, so you can provide knowledgeable support for other musicians in that area. If you like violin, or have a friend who is a violinist, learn to play the standard literature for violin and piano. You thus garner a reputation among violinists for being an expert collaborator for them to call on. You could apply the same thinking in any number of areas: solo vocal literature, operatic excerpts, viola, violoncello, and several wind or brass instruments, such as flute, clarinet, trumpet, or trombone. A special version of collaboration is that of providing the piano reduction of the orchestra part in the piano concerto literature. If you build a reputation for knowing the "second piano" for most of the standard piano concerto repertoire, you will be hired constantly to provide support at school recitals, piano festivals, and competitions where concerto performance is required.

Success story: A young woman learned all the flute and piano repertoire during her graduate studies. After leaving school, she moved to an urban area and within a few months became the collaborator of choice for every professional flutist in the city and enjoyed a busy schedule playing this repertoire in performances, competitions, studio classes, and rehearsals.

- Become a music technology geek. Know about and keep up with software for sequencing, arranging, orchestration, or setting up a basic piano lab. Expertise in this area gets out of date rapidly, so once you learn the basics, you will have the ongoing task of keeping up with the newest developments. Musicians at all levels increasingly depend on technology for heretofore time-consuming and labor-intensive tasks. Knowing what's available and how to use it are assets you can market and get paid to teach. Moreover, you might be surprised at the number of college job searches that give priority to candidates who have technology skills.

Success story: A young woman was hired right out of college to run the education department of a major manufacturer of music technology equipment. Her job is to be a liaison between the company she works for and music professionals: pianists, composers, and arrangers. She often appears on programs at music conventions to introduce company products, and in demonstrating ends up doing a considerable amount of piano performance.

- A thriving offshoot of music technology is that of music for computer games. This area is highly volatile and commercial, so it is apt to be all-consuming, but for those who are expert, it can be very profitable.

Success stories: A young man as a college senior was hired to create music for the newest edition of a best-selling computer game and had a job waiting for him the day he graduated.

A second success story came as a surprise to the college student who improvised a piano arrangement of the music used in a popular computer game. He put it up on YouTube, and it quickly garnered thousands of hits. Now computer game companies fly him everywhere in the world to appear live in performances of a menu of popular computer game music. Fans cheer him on like a rock star.

- Develop your skills as a conductor, so you can lead both small instrumental ensembles and choirs. Many church musicians, for example, need to conduct choral groups regularly and instrumental ensembles on special occasions.

Success story: A young woman worked part-time as a church choir accompanist during her college years for a well-known denomination. Her skills filtered through the church grapevine, so she was offered a full-time position as minister of music of a large church in a nearby metropolitan area.

- Become an expert in church music, focusing on liturgy of two or three specific denominations, so you become an attractive candidate for church positions, especially for those denominations for which you are a specialist.

Success story: A young man was offered a position at a church-affiliated university precisely because he knew the music used in weekly on-campus worship services.

- Develop skills as a piano entertainer. Whether you find pleasure in jazz, pop, New Age, show tunes, or some combination of these, learning to improvise your own arrangements qualifies you for jobs at many public venues, such as hotel lobbies, shopping malls, and restaurants. Moreover, if you move in this direction, you will undoubtedly develop your improvisation and arranging techniques. Organize how to teach these skills to others, and you will generate a large clientele for your teaching studio or be in demand to teach these skills in a classroom.

Success stories: A young man started as a casual-listening pianist in the lobby of a major hotel chain and garnered such a following that the company's executives arranged for him to tour as a featured artist in their hotels throughout the world.

A second success story: A young woman received her master of music in piano performance, but, because she loved to improvise and play popular music, she sustained a successful international career entertaining in casual settings: hotels, restaurants, cruise ships, resorts. At a Swiss ski resort, she was lucky enough to be heard by a recording executive, who

offered her a contract that resulted over the years in more than a dozen recordings and one Grammy nomination. When she reached a point in her
career where she no longer wanted to tour, she settled with her family in
an urban area. A local college soon contacted her to teach improvisation
courses. Soon her college teaching overflowed into demand for private
lessons in improvisation.

- There is an administrative staff behind the scenes of every musical
  presentation and every musical organization. Explore becoming
  an intern for one of these administrative support groups while
  you are still in school. Not only will you learn administrative and
  managerial skills, but you also will lay the groundwork for future
  employment. Many of these organizations prefer to hire staff
  members who have studied music and understand the profession
  from a performance standpoint. You may resist the idea of relegating your role to being backstage rather than in the spotlight.
  But by doing so, you can learn a great deal about the music business that will be extremely helpful in promoting your own career.
  Moreover, you do so while being a part of the team that presents
  music to the public.

Success story: A young pianist worked summers during his college
years as a staff member of a large summer music festival. When he graduated, he was hired as part of the year-round staff for the same festival.
A few years later, he successfully applied for the position of managing a
much larger summer festival. Finally, he became the manager of one of
the most famous symphony orchestras. Did he give up playing the piano?
Not at all. He was known throughout his career as a fine pianist and was
presented with many opportunities to perform.

Does pursuing ancillary fields mean you give up learning and playing the classical repertoire? Not if you don't want to. You will find plenty
of opportunities to present yourself as a classical pianist, working your
performances into the fabric of your overall job-related activities, as well
as performances in your community if you reach out for them. Your

reputation as a fine pianist will grow with every performance, and one successful performance will almost always generate other performance opportunities.

Remember that no one can create your career profile except you. This responsibility might seem onerous to you at the beginning, but keep in mind that as an individual you possess your own special mix of strengths and interests. What you have to offer is a reflection of you, no one else. Keep underscoring that concept until it becomes an integral part of your very being, and know that once you develop a firm belief in your own power and individuality, the specific ideas as to how to apply those strengths will follow.

17

The Road Ahead

A young pianist was invited to perform at a benefit concert in a private home. As he entered the home, he could not help but admire its opulence. Grand marble arches surrounded a great living room where expensive furniture and art pieces were on display. The piano sat in front of graceful sets of French doors that looked out onto a magnificent garden with fountains and a swimming pool. Mountains loomed picturesquely in the background.

Overwhelmed, the pianist uttered a small cry of admiration, but said, "Guess I chose the wrong profession, after all." This comment reflects historical evidence that musicians typically have not been among the most affluent members of any society. Over two centuries ago, musicians were employees of or supported by powerful, wealthy individuals or institutions, often nobility or the church. As these hierarchies declined, musicians had to seek their livelihood by performing services, such as entertaining audiences or teaching students. For most musicians, these roles were not profitable enough to result in a lavish lifestyle. Despite a handful of exceptions, musicians in general had to be satisfied with a less extravagant material existence. The trade-off, of course, was that they spent their lives working with something they adored, their very reason for being . . . music.

After the performance, the aforementioned young pianist found himself in a conversation with his host, the owner of the magnificent mansion that was so overwhelming. The host fell into a brief reverie, obviously moved by the music he had heard. He recalled that when he was young, he had wanted more than anything else to play the guitar, an instrument he still loved. But his parents had persuaded him to do something more "practical." He chose engineering because it was "easy" for him and offered jobs that "paid lots of money." Then he said, "Now that I have taken early retirement, maybe I can take up the guitar and at last do what I've always wanted to do. Do you think it's too late for me?"

To be sure, we should acknowledge that many engineers love what they do, and would not share the sentiments of the man in this story. But, if you were born with the soul of a musician, as apparently this man was, being deterred from following your dream because the profession is financially modest at best and uncertain at worst is a mistake. You should do all you can to live your life doing what gives you joy and satisfaction. For when you near the end of your existence on this earth, you want to be able to look back with a sense of fulfillment and peace.

But at this point in your life, you are looking ahead, not back. Enjoy the prospects that are before you with energy and excitement. Think of the repertoire you want to learn! Think of the places you want to play! Think of the musicians you want to collaborate with! Think of the groups of people, including oldsters and children, you want to move, to inspire, to give pleasure to! And above all, think of yourself loving every minute of it through the years!

You must continue to treat the gift you have been given with respect and love. You have offered your time, energy, work, and imagination to this talent, developing it to the highest level possible. You will continue to do so. At this point, you need to turn your thinking not to what this talent can *get* for you, but rather to what you can *give* with it.

Almost every religious or philosophical system in the world, whether old or new, has espoused the principle that whenever you turn your attention to giving, to sharing, to reaching out to your fellow human beings, you will be rewarded with returns many times over. Many bodies of thought continue to exhort you to have faith that this metaphysical principle will indeed operate, and to proceed accordingly. At points in your life when the future seems uncertain, having this kind of faith may be difficult. But your choice is either to believe in your future and revel in its possibilities, or to doubt your future and harbor insecurity and fear. It is not a hard choice to make logically, but implementing it is sometimes tough.

Faith is fueled by action. Dream your dreams and enjoy the exhilaration they generate, but also take steps to bring them into being, holding positive thoughts as you do.

- Do you have business cards? If not, create them online inexpensively, order them, and be quick to use them.
- Is your résumé up to date and professional looking, ready to send out? If not, or if you do not know how to construct it, seek guidance from a teacher, get it ready, and keep it current.
- Do you have recordings of your performances, CDs or DVDs, ready to hand out or send? Are they attractively packaged, and do they include biographical information?
- Do you have a website that presents you as a professional musician?
- Are you on a professional online network?
- Are any of your performances on YouTube?
- Do you know the agencies that can help you find job openings in fields you are qualified for?
- Do you conduct regular online searches in areas that might offer you opportunities?
- Do you know the libraries, museums, schools, or other institutions in your area that offer concert series or instructional programs? Have you contacted them with your professional information and a specific program suggestion?

- Do you belong to professional musicians' organizations that provide information about job openings and in which you can network?

Such activities may seem mundane or distastefully commercial when compared with the rarefied, esoteric world of the artist. And, indeed, the two worlds are quite separate, so you can be active in both without sullying either. And remember that no matter how wonderful and rewarding your musical product may be, you will enjoy it alone if you do not let others know about it.

Also remember that it is a busy world out there, each person pursuing individual interests and goals. Do not expect to be greeted with adulation or even interest, just because you manage to get someone's attention. In fact, you will be shrugged off most of the time, sometimes politely, sometimes not. Condition yourself not to take it personally. Regard building your career as you would a difficult passage you are trying to learn at the keyboard. You know you won't be able to play it securely up to speed until a lot of groundwork has been laid. Similarly, you probably won't be able to make the professional connections you want until you have laid the groundwork, in this case getting your presence known. Serendipity is created by planning, action, and persistence.

Use your imagination to create markets for your talents. Concerts do not always take place in concert halls. Teaching does not always take place in schools. Yesterday's patterns of consumption went out of style at sundown. Today's demands for your talent are for today only. Tomorrow you must create ideas to meet tomorrow's demands. Your talent and work have prepared you for the career you want, now use them to build the career itself.

The road ahead is a glorious adventure. Love it and live it.

ANNOTATED SELECTED BIBLIOGRAPHY

The following bibliography is a guide for both suggested reading and building a professional library. Thus it references recent books, as well as some that have become famous among pianists over the past decades. Obviously, it will take time to explore this list, perhaps years, but a blueprint of reading and reference material early in your development is valuable. Make collecting professional books, reading them, and referring to them a part of your musical life, even if doing so means taking time from the more easily accessible information and entertainment offered by electronic devices. Remember that books often present ideas and develop concepts not typically found in more expedient media.

THE PIANO AND PIANISTS

Dubal, David. *Reflections from the Keyboard: The World of the Concert Pianist.* New York: Summit Books, Simon and Schuster, 1984.

This volume is a collection of thirty-five interviews with the most celebrated concert pianists of the twentieth century. The author's insights into the challenges and rewards of being a classical concert pianist are reflected in both the style and substance of the dialogues.

Dubal, David. *The Art of the Piano: Its Performers, Literature, and Recordings.* 3rd ed. Pompton Plains, NJ: Amadeus Press, 2004.

This is an annotated reference volume. The first alphabetical listing is of pianists, both past and present; the second of well-known piano literature, arranged by composer. An addendum to this edition includes both pianists and composers not mentioned in earlier editions. This is a useful book for short reference information.

Loesser, Arthur. *Men, Women, and Pianos: A Social History.* Mineola, NY: Dover, 1990.

This paperback edition is a reprint of the 1954 original. It is famous throughout the piano world as a highly entertaining history of the piano and its celebrated practitioners. Reading it provides an easy, enjoyable way of learning a great deal about the piano and the art of playing it.

Schoenberg, Harold. *The Great Pianists from Mozart to the Present*. New York: Simon and Schuster, 1963.

The author presents an informative, historical account of the piano and highly reputed pianists. The book examines the evolution of the piano, the personalities who played it, and the methods of playing and teaching it, all in a lively and often amusing style.

PIANO TECHNIQUE

Developing pianists can become confused when reading books about piano technique, for approaches as to the best way to master playing the piano often differ, and most pedagogues present personal methodology as gospel. Still, exploring a variety of ideas about piano technique encourages flexibility and often opens avenues that help solve technical problems.

Banowetz, Joseph. *The Pianist's Guide to Pedaling*. Bloomington: Indiana University Press, 1965. (First Midland Book Edition, 1992).

The first part of this book deals with a history of the piano's pedals and describes techniques for using the three pedals usually found on today's instruments. The second part applies pedal techniques to a selection of well-known composers, with contributing chapters by Dean Elder, Mark Hanson, Maurice Hinson, and William S. Newman.

Bernstein, Seymour. *With Your Own Two Hands*. New York: Schirmer Books, 1981.

The author holds the premise that preparing and performing music is a catalyst for achieving wholeness of one's psyche. He then explores motivation, concentration, and movement at the keyboard in the context of specific musical passages, as well as memorizing, and performance anxiety.

Fink, Seymour. *Mastering Piano Technique: A Guide for Students, Teachers, and Performers*. Portland, OR: Amadeus Press, 1992.

After defining the role of physical movement at the keyboard in relation to musical and expressive goals, the author analyzes various physical movements often used at the keyboard and offers exercises designed to perfect and incorporate each. He then applies these movements to various passages in well-known keyboard pieces.

Gat, Josef. *The Technique of Piano Playing*. 2nd ed. Trans. by István Klezky. London: Collet's Holdings, 1965.

This is a landmark work by a celebrated professor of Budapest's Liszt Academy. The author explores the gamut of physical complexities inherent in playing piano music, emphasizing flexibility with a series of film clips of famous pianists playing well-known musical passages. He includes a series of body exercises to achieve flexibility and stay in shape.

Gerig, Reginald. *Famous Pianists and Their Technique*. 2nd ed. Bloomington: Indiana University Press, 2007.

The author presents a historical survey of pedagogical methods for the piano from their earliest appearance through the twentieth century. Methods are described, and frequently original text is quoted, sometimes in significant segments. This book offers an impressive, extensive survey of its subject.

Gieseking, Walter, and Karl Leimer. *Piano Technique*. Mineola, NY: Dover, 1976.

Two earlier books are bound together in one volume: *The Shortest Way to Pianistic Perfection* (1930), and *Rhythmics, Dynamics, Pedal and Other Problems of Piano Playing* (1938). Gieseking was one of the most celebrated pianists of the early twentieth century, and Leimer was his teacher. This approach is well known for its detailed presentation of learning to play a piece by studying it away from the piano, as well as a physical approach that is based on flexibility of the shoulders and upper arms.

Kochevitsky, George. *The Art of Piano Playing: A Scientific Approach*. Miami: Summy Birchard, 1967.

The author presents the role of the central nervous system as fundamental in secure piano playing. He leads up to his thesis with a short historical survey of selected pianists and pedagogues. The information he imparts is worth wading through despite a style some have found difficult to read.

Mark, Thomas. *What Every Pianist Should Know about the Body: With Supplemental Material for Organists by Roberta Gary and Thom Miles*. Chicago: Gia Publications, 2004.

Pianists who suffer from physical problems especially value this clear presentation of the body's anatomy in relation to piano playing. Pianists who undertake studying this material may prevent injury.

Neuhaus, Heinrich. *The Art of Piano Playing*. Trans. K. A. Leibovitch. Chicago: Independent Publishers Group, Kahn and Averill, 1998.

Neuhaus taught many of the most celebrated Russian pianists of the mid-twentieth century. In this volume he presents wisdom gathered from years of effective teaching rather than an organized piano method. Despite its anecdotal approach, this book enjoys the deserved reputation of being both informative and inspiring.

Onishi, Aiko. *Pianism*. N.p.: Anima Press, 2009.

The author covers a broad range of topics: tone production, rotation as a component of technique, practicing procedures, and interpretive development. Although the volume is slim, it contains many concepts that pianists have found both valuable and practical.

Schwiebert, Jerald. *Physical Expression and the Performing Artist: Moving beyond the Plateau*. Ann Arbor: University of Michigan Press, 2011.

This book offers a compendium of techniques drawn from hatha yoga, t'ai chi, Pilates, Rolfing, Alexander, Feldenkrais, Laban, and Stanislavski. Anatomical drawings enhance awareness of inefficient movement, and the author offers exercises to achieve maximum efficiency in all movement-based performances.

Whiteside, Abby. *On Piano Playing*. Portland, OR: Amadeus Press, 1997.

This anthology combines earlier writings by the author: *Indispensables of Piano Playing* (1955) and *Mastering the Chopin Etudes and Other Essays* (1969). Whiteside represents the epitome of whole-body solutions to the challenges of piano playing, an approach that, although provocative, many professional pianists endorse.

PREPARATION AND PERFORMANCE

Bruser, Madeline. *The Art of Practicing*. New York: Bell Tower, 1997. (Paperback, Random House, New York, 1999).

The author explores in detail physical and mental attitudes toward practicing. The volume includes photographs of efficient physical positions for playing most musical instruments. Subjects such as stimulating imagination, avoiding fatigue, and memorization are also addressed. The text includes many anecdotes about professional musicians.

Gordon, Stewart. *Mastering the Art of Performance: A Primer for Musicians*. New York: Oxford University Press, 2006.

Performance is defined, and many aspects of it are addressed, including evaluation of you as the performer, preparation, organization, practice techniques, memorization, stage fright, evaluation after performance, and lifelong challenges performers face.

Greene, Don. *Performance Success: Performing Your Best under Pressure*. New York: Routledge, 2002.

Based on a course given at the Juilliard School of Music, the author begins by asking the reader to take a survey of 100 questions designed to clarify the reader's attitude toward performance. The survey is typical of the author's method throughout the book, for worksheets of various types are interspersed with advice.

Klickstein, Gerald. *The Musician's Way: A Guide to Practice, Performance, and Wellness.* New York: Oxford University Press, 2009.

The author offers suggestions for practicing, memorizing, performance anxiety control, injury prevention, and career planning. Valuable ideas are presented in a clear, direct style with a businesslike approach.

Maisel, Eric. *Performance Anxiety.* 2nd ed. New York: Watson Guptill, 2005.

The first part of this book explores various manifestations of performance anxiety. The second part offers techniques for addressing and controlling it, including calming exercises, autosuggestion techniques, and long-term management.

Ristad, Eloise. *A Soprano on Her Head: Right-Side-Up Reflections on Life and Other Performances.* Moah, UT: Real People Press, 1982.

This book is a classic among books that offer advice on how to achieve successful performance. Enjoyable and easy to read, it addresses performance anxiety solutions and explores overall attitudes toward artistic endeavors.

Snyder, Bob. *Music and Memory: An Introduction.* Cambridge, MA, Massachusetts Institute of Technology, 2000.

The first section of this book relates memorizing to cognitive psychology and linguistics. The second section focuses on how the presented concepts can be applied to music. This is a valuable in-depth study, but it is not for the reader seeking a quick "how-to" presentation.

Willimon, Aaron. *Musical Excellence: Strategies and Techniques to Enhance Performance.* New York: Oxford University Press, 2004.

This is a collection of articles by many authors covering a broad range of topics: the physical demands of performance, measuring performance, strategies for practicing, memorizing, sight-reading, and improvising. Also included are discussions of physical fitness, Alexander technique, various psychological feedbacks, with even a chapter on drugs and musical performance.

ANCILLARY SKILLS

Chung, Brian, and Dennis Thurmond. *Improvisation at the Piano: A Systematic Approach for the Classically Trained Pianist.* Van Nuys, CA: Alfred Publishing, 2007.

Written for pianists who have never attempted to improvise, this book offers a step-by-step approach, starting with simple exercises and progressing to complex improvisation. Its approach includes improvisation in all styles historically significant in Western music. Its format is that of a workbook, with many musical examples and exercises.

Gregorich, Shellie, and Benjamin Moritz. *Keyboard Skills for Music Educators: Score Reading.* New York: Routledge, 2012.

The authors provide a gradual, graded approach to open score reading, from two-part through multiple-part scores, incorporating a variety of clefs. Musical examples are drawn from the choral and instrumental repertoire ranging from Renaissance to contemporary works.

Katz, Martin. *The Complete Collaborator: The Pianist as Partner.* New York: Oxford University Press, 2009.

Written in a direct, often witty style, this book is authored by one of the most celebrated collaborative pianists. It covers the complete gamut: collaboration with instrumentalists and singers, ensemble precision, balance, languages, breathing, and orchestral collaboration. Audio examples are available on a companion website.

COLLEGE ADMISSIONS AND LIFE

Cohen, Harlan. *The Naked Roomate: And 107 Other Issues You May Run Into in College.* Naperville, IL: Sourcebooks, 2009.

This is a witty, readable, and often irreverent look at college life. It covers many topics, including traditional academic challenges and current social patterns. It is likely to appeal more to students than to their parents.

Holly, Rich. *Majoring in Music: All the Stuff You Need to Know.* Galesville, MD: Meredith Music Publications, 2009.

The author offers advice on academic, musical, and social matters for music majors at a college or university. The author's writing style is direct, and the suggestions are practical.

Korn, Rachael, ed. *How to Survive Getting into College.* Atlanta: Hundreds of Heads Books, 2006.

This is a compilation of advice gathered from high school and college students, as well as parents. It is easy to read. Although its information may be only partly applicable to any individual, most readers will garner some helpful ideas from it.

Tanabe, Gen, and Kelly Tanabe. *Get Into Any College: Secrets of Harvard Students*. 4th ed. Los Alto, CA: SuperCollege LLC, 2004.

This is a "how-to" manual that advises students on a wide variety of topics: choosing colleges, doing well on tests, handling interviews, and applying for scholarships. It is for the general student, although music students will find much useful information in it.

Wilkining, David. *How to Get into the Top Graduate Schools: What You Need to Know about Getting into Law, Medical, and Other Ivy League Schools Explained Simply*. Ocala, FL: Atlantic Publishing Group, 2008.

This book is specialized, as its title suggests. Its information is helpful to all those applying for graduate schools, not merely those mentioned in its title. It covers such topics as how to select graduate schools, meet deadlines, take tests, and apply for scholarships.

CAREER DEVELOPMENT

Baskerville, David, and Tim Baskerville. *Music Business Handbook and Career Guide*. 9th ed. Thousand Oaks, CA: Sage, 2010.

This well-known, classic survey addresses all segments of the overall music industry. Its focus is primarily on commercial aspects of music, particularly those aimed to garner a broad popular market. Even so, it can serve to broaden horizons for classical musicians and provide practical details about music as a business.

Beeching, Angela Myles. *Beyond Talent: Creating a Successful Career in Music* New York. Oxford University Press, 2010.

The author offers far-reaching insights into building a professional profile in today's musical environment. The book is relevant for those whose focus is classical music, addressing both practical and philosophical issues with a realistic yet positive outlook.

Radbill, Catherine Fitterman. *Introduction to The Music Industry: An Entrepreneurial Approach*. New York: Routledge, 2013.

The author encourages creative thinking in forging career profiles and addresses aspects of the music industry, including issues of copyright, touring, recording, publishing, and digital music services. All subjects are illustrated by case studies. The book is oriented toward musicians who seek success in various popular music areas, but classically trainted musicians can still glean valuable information from its contents, especially the author's discussions of how to adopt a creative, out-of-the-box mindset for career planning.

PIANO LITERATURE

Gillespie, John. *Five Centuries of Keyboard Literature*. Mineola, NY: Dover, 1978. (A reprint of the 1965 original published by Wadsworth Publishing.)

This is one of several textbooks used in college-level courses devoted to surveying keyboard literature. It is well organized and easy to read.

Gordon, Stewart. *A History of Keyboard Literature: Music for the Piano and Its Forerunners*. Belmont, CA: Wadsworth Group/Thompson Learning, 1996.

This is one of several textbooks used in college-level courses devoted to surveying keyboard literature. Written by a pianist, it details many works, including each sonata of Haydn, Mozart, Beethoven, and Schubert. It also includes important works written up until the early 1990s.

Hinson, Maurice. *Guide to the Pianist's Repertoire*. 3rd ed. Bloomington: Indiana University Press, 2000.

This volume presents an annotated list of well-known and little-known piano repertoire from the past three and a half centuries, alphabetized by composer. Publishers and available editions of older music are presented, as well as commentary about style, effect, and difficulty. This is an essential piano literature dictionary for many professionals.

Hinson, Maurice, and Wesley Roberts. *The Piano in Chamber Ensemble: An Annotated Guide*. 2nd ed. Bloomington: Indiana University Press, 2006.

A companion to Hinson's solo repertoire guide, this volume divides the collaborative literature involving piano into different instrumental groups. For each combination the authors provide an annotated listing of works, alphabetized by composer. It is an essential dictionary of works involving the piano in collaboration with other instruments.

Kirby, F. E. *Music for Piano: a short history*. Portland, OR: Amadeus Press, 1995, corrected revision 2000. (An updated reprint of the 1966 original published by Schirmer Books.)

This is one of several books used in college-level courses devoted to surveying the history of keyboard literature. Written by a music historian, it emphasizes the historical perspective of the music under consideration.

INDEX

accentuation, 33–34
administration, 157
Albéniz, Isaac, 131, 144
Alcotts, 86
Alkan, Charles–Valentin, 148
anxiety. *See* performance, psychological preparation
arms. *See* physical approach
Andersen, Hans Christian, 7
Arensky, Anton Stepanovich, 148
arpeggios, 32–33

Bach, Carl Philipp Emanuel, 140
Bach, Johann Christian, 147
Bach, Johann Sebastian, 3, 6, 9, 45, 60, 84, 87, 131, 132, 133, 134, 139, 152
Barber, Samuel, 135, 147
Bartók, Béla, 2, 3, 32, 39, 131, 145, 152
Baudelaire, Charles Pierre, 86, 87
Beethoven, Ludwig van, 2, 6, 45, 78, 84, 104, 131, 132, 133, 135, 140, 152
Berg, Alban, 146
Berlioz, Hector, 6, 153
Bertrand, Aloysius, 86
Bischoff, Hans, 139
Bizet, Georgs, 46
Blavatsky, Helena Petrovna, 87
Böcklin, Arnold, 86
Bolcolm, William, 39, 148
Boulanger, Nadia, 103
Boulez, Pierre, 146

Brahms, Johannes, 9, 35, 85, 103, 131, 135, 141, 142, 153
Buddha, 61
Burgmüller, Johann Friedrich Franz, 35
business cards, 163
Busoni, Ferruccio, 139, 148
Byron, George Gordon. *See* Lord Byron

Cage, John, 148
career planning, 128–129
Carter, Elliott, 148
Chaminade, Cécile, 148
Chopin, Frédéric, 3, 4, 35, 37, 60, 78, 84, 105, 108, 131, 135, 141, 152
Chorley, H. F., 105
church music, 157
Clementi, Muzio, 10, 37, 141
colaboration
    benefits of, 47, 136
    repertoire, 155
    teacher's attitude toward, 18
    See also listening, colaboratively
college
    academic record, 117–119
    auditions, 117
    campus types, 114–116
    financial aid, 119–120
    friendships, 126
    language requirements, 119
competitions. *See* repertoire, competition
computer game music, 156

concert–going, 127
conducting, 156
Confucius, 7
Copland, Aaron, 6, 147
Corigliano, John, 39, 149
Couperin, François, 138
Cowell, Henry, 149
Cramer, Johann Baptist, 35, 37
Creston, Paul, 39
Crumb, George, 149
cultural opportunities, 127
Czerny, Carl, 9, 17, 35, 36–37, 139, 141

Dante, 85
Da Ponte, Lorenzo, 87
Debussy, Claude, 38, 84, 86, 87, 88, 89,
        131, 133, 134, 142–143, 153
Delius, Frederick, 6
Dello Joio, Norman, 147
Delphi, 86
Dohnányi, Ernst von, 17, 35, 148
Dussek, Jan Ladislav, 147
Dutilleux, Henri, 149
Dvořák, Antonin, 145

Eastman School of Music, 32
Emerson, Ralph Waldo, 7, 86
emotional projection
    achievement of, 84–89
    importance of, 81–83
    influenced by, 83–84
English. See college, language requirements
etudes, 37–39
Evans, Bill, 46
evalutaion. See performance, evaluation

Fauré, Gabriel, 142, 152, 153
Faye, Amy, 98
Fétis, François–Joseph, 38
Field, John, 141
figured bass realization, 47
Finney, Ross Lee, 149
Franck, César, 145, 152
Froberger, Johann Jaokb, 147
fund raising. See grant writing

Genhart, Cécile, 32
Gershwin, George, 103
Gibran, Kahlil, 7
Gieseking, Walter, 95
Ginastera, Alberto, 144
Goethe, Johann Wolfgang von, 85, 87
grades. See college, academic record
Gradus ad Parnassum, 37
Granados, Enrique, 131, 144
grant writing, 154
Gretchaninov, Alexander, 10
Grieg, Edvard, 145
Griffes, Charles Tomlinson, 86
Gurlitt, Cornelius, 35

Handel, George Frideric, 139
Hanon, Charles–Louis, 17, 35, 36
Hartmann, Victor, 86
Hawthorne, Nathaniel, 86
Haydn, Franz Joseph, 2, 132, 140, 152
Hebbel, Christian Friedrich, 85
Heine, Heinrich, 87
Heller, Stephen, 35, 37, 148
Hensel, Fanny Mendelssohn, 147
Henselt, Adolf von, 148
Herder, Johann Gottfried, 85
Hiller, Ferdinand, 148
Hindemith, Paul, 145, 152
Hoffman, E. T. A., 85
Horowitz, Vladimir, 46
Hugo, Victor, 7, 85
Hummel, Johann Nepomuk, 141

improvisation
    benefits of, 45–46
    teaching, 19
    techniques and exercises, 51–55
Inkermann, Otto. See Sternau, C. O.
inner hearing. See listening, inner hearing
Ives, Charles, 11, 39, 86, 147

Janáček, Leoš, 145
Jean Paul. See Richter, Jean Paul
Jesus Christ, 61
Juilliard School of Music, 129, 151

Kabalevsky, Dmitri Borisovich, 143
Kapell, William, 21–24, 151
Kapustin, Nikolai, 39
Kirkpatrick, Ralph, 138

Landor, Walter Savage, 7
Lao Tzu, 6
Liebermann, Lowell, 149
Ligeti, György, 39, 149
listening
    across the repertoire, 74–76
    collboratively, 72–74
    inner hearing, 76–79
    to yourself, 71–72
List, Eugene, 151
Liszt, Franz, 9, 33–34, 38, 45, 85, 88, 91,
    98, 131, 135, 141, 142, 152, 153
Longfellow, Hanry Wadsworth, 7
Longo, Alessandro, 138
Lord Byron, 85
Luther, Martin, 87
Lyapunov, Sergei Mikhailovich, 148

MacDowell, Edward, 37, 89, 147
Mallarmé, Stéphane, 87
management. See administration
Martin, Frank, 149
Martino, Donald, 149
Marvin, Frederick, 138
Mason, William, 33–34
Massenet, Jules, 148
Medtner, Nikolai Karlovich, 132, 143–144
memorization
    drills, 96–98
    reasons for, 92–93
    types of, 94–96
Mendelssohn, Fanny. See Hensel, Fanny
    Mendelssohn
Mendelssohn, Felix, 9, 131, 141, 153
Menuhin, Yehudi, 6
Messiaen, Olivier, 39, 88, 142–143, 152
Metastasio, 87
metronome, 34
Michelangelo, 85
Miekiewicz, Adam Bernard, 87

Moiseiwitsch, Benno, 86
Mompou, Federico, 132, 144
Moscheles, Ignaz, 38, 147
Moszkowski, Moritz, 35, 37, 148
Mozart, Wolfgang Amadeus, 2, 9, 45, 60,
    81, 84, 108, 131, 132, 140, 152
Muczynski, Robert, 149
Mugellini, Bruno, 139
Müller, Wilhelm, 87
Musorgsky, Modest Petrovich, 86, 143

Napoleon Bonaparte, 2
Nebra, Manuel Blasco de, 147
negativism. See performance, psychological
    preparation
nervousness. See performance, pschological
    preparation
Nietzsche, Friedrich, 7

online network, 163

Paganini, Nicolò, 91
pedagogy. See teacher, training
performance
    evaluation, 65–66
    teacher's attitude toward, 18
    professions that require, 58
    psychological preparation, 59–64
Persichetti, Vincent, 147
Peterson, Oscar, 39, 46
Petrarch, Francesco, 85
physical approach, 33–34
Plato, 7
playing by ear, 77–78
Ponte. See Da Ponte, Lorenzo
popular styles, 157
Poulenc, Francis, 9, 142
practice
    away from the piano, 77
    balancing with life's activities, 25–27
    building schedules, 27–29, 124–125
    teaching good habits, 18
    techniques to sustain attention, 72
Prix de Rome, 106
professional organizations, 164

profile. *See* career planning
Prokofiev, Sergey Sergeyevich, 39, 131, 135, 143

Rachmaninoff, Sergei Vasilievich, 6, 38–39, 86, 89, 105, 131, 135, 143, 153
Rafael, 85
Raff, Joachim, 148
Rameau, Jean–Philippe, 88, 138
Ravel, Maurice, 86, 88, 103, 106, 131, 133, 135, 142–143, 153
reading. *See* sight reading
Reger, Max, 145
Régnier, Henri de, 86
recordings, 163
repertoire
    competition, 135–136
    contemporary, 132–133
    content of, 135
    difficulty of, 134–135
    exploring, 131–132
    reviewing, 134
    teaching, 18
résumé, 163
Richter, Jean Paul, 8
Rimsky–Korsakov, Nicolai Andreyevich, 12
Roman Catholic Church, 87
Rosenfeld, Paul, 105
Roussel, Albert, 12
Rubinstein, Anton Grigor'yevich, 148
Rubinstein, Nikolay Grigor'yevich, 104

Saint Francis of Assisi, 88
Saint Francis of Paola, 88
Saint–Saëns, Camile, 106, 148
Samaroff, Olga, 21–24, 65, 129, 151
scales, 32
Scarlatti, Domenico, 131, 138
schedules. *See* practice
scholarships. *See* college, financial aid
score reduction, 47
Schikaneder, Emanuel, 87
Schiller, Johann Christoph von, 87
Schönberg, Arnold, 146, 152
Schubert, Franz, 10, 131, 141, 142

Schumann, Clara, 92, 105, 148
Schumann, Robert, 10, 85, 87, 88, 89, 105, 131, 141, 153
Scriabin, Alexander Nikolayevich, 38, 131, 143–144
Senancour, Etienne Pivert de, 85
Sharp, William, 86
Shostakovich, Dmitri Dmitrievich, 143
sight reading
    benefits of, 46, 51
    teaching, 19
    types and techniques, 48–51
Smetana, Biedrich, 145
speed. *See* tempo
Soler, Antonio, 138
Sousa, John Philip, 46
Sternau, C. O., 85
Stockhausen, Karlheinz, 12, 146
Stravinsky, Igor Fyodorovich, 10, 39, 152
Szymanowski, Karol, 39, 132, 145

Takemitsu, Toru, 149
Tatum, Art, 46
Tchaikovsky, Peter Ilyich, 104, 135
teacher
    changing, 19–21
        college–level, 112–114
        training, 153
technique
    acquiring through repertoire, 40–41
    attitude toward, 31
    teaching, 17
technology, 155–156
tempo, 34
theory
    teacher's attitude toward, 18–19
Thomson, Virgil, 6
Thoreau, Henry David, 7, 86
TOEFL (Test of English as a Foreign Language). *See* college, language requirements
tone
    teaching, 17
    quality of piano, 17

torso. *See* physical approach
transposition, 47
Tureck, Rosalyn, 151
Turina, Joachín, 144

university, *See* college

Verlaine, Paul–Marie, 87
Villa–Lobos, Heitor, 89, 144
Vine, Carl, 149
Viñes, Ricardo, 132–133

Watteau, Jean–Antoine, 86
Weber, Carl Maria von, 141
Webern, Anton, 146
website, 163
Wieck, Friedrich, 92
wrists. *See* physical approach
writing, 154

Xenakis, Iannis, 12

You Tube, 163